Gender Disparity in UK Jazz –

A Discussion

By Sammy Stein

Edited by Debbie Burke

Published by Amazon KDP

Gender Disparity in UK Jazz – A Discussion

ISBN: 9798552101008

Copyright 2020 Sammy Stein

Edited by Debbie Burke/Queen Esther Publishing LLC

DISCLAIMER: This is a work of nonfiction. It contains research, interviews, facts and figures as well as opinions from both experts and laypeople. Although the author has made every effort to ensure that the information in this book was correct at press time, she does not assume and hereby disclaims any liability to any party for any loss, damage, or disruption caused by errors or omissions, whether such errors or omissions result from negligence, accident, or any other cause.

For my Dad, who died whilst this book was being written. Dad taught me to be always curious, to always climb that extra peak because the view from the top is amazing, to plant with great care and attention to detail and that it is always OK to stand by your passions.

TABLE OF CONTENTS

Introduction

Interviewing women for my previous books, "All That's Jazz" (Tomahawk Press) and "Women in Jazz" (8th House), as well as discussions with many female performers, have given me a privileged and unique insight into the collective experiences they have had on the jazz scene and their impact. The disparity between men and women in jazz often comes up as a topic of conversation. Undoubtedly, progress has been made over the last few decades and there are many men and women who support each other on an equal basis. However, there remains work to be done and there are issues which we still need to tackle head on and try to resolve.

This book looks specifically at UK jazz and includes quantitative and qualitative data as well as anecdotal evidence which reflects the experience of female performers.

UK jazz is a beautiful thing. Historically influenced by the traditional jazz, swing and bop music which came from across the Atlantic and by the vibrant cultures of the near continent of Europe, UK jazz musicians have added their own unique touches. These enriched the already multi-cultural essences of jazz which made their way to the UK. The Europeans added a dose of defiance after World War II and again during the 1960s when young players rebelled against the deplorable actions of the generations before and the social mores of the time. Aspects of Scandinavian music have also been assimilated into the art form. The quintessential jazz scene of this small island nation has an influence across the globe.

Each element slots together to create the allure of the music. The expression in melody, rhythm and improvisation reflect UK society as it changes politically and socially. The UK is justly proud of its eclectic scene and the fact that good quality jazz music can be heard in small and larger venues.

The UK jazz scene is blistering with more people appreciating the music. Only a decade ago UK jazz had lost its lustre and become enveloped in apathy. It was sinking, its spirit waning. Then came the revival of recent years led by young people who discovered jazz and brought with them an energy which re-invigorated the fading scene. The quality of music now is astounding and well worth turning out for, whether it is a sunny outdoor gig or one in a crowded club on a dark winter's evening and, regardless of the restrictions placed upon it due to the COVID pandemic or any future unforeseen events, jazz persists and will endure.

Yet look closer. Where are the women? Why are there few women in audiences or on stage? From past recordings and reviews, we know there have been incredible women who, as part of the UK jazz legacy, set venues alight with their innovative performances. However, check the jazz archives and photographic collections which document UK jazz and it is hard to find female musicians. Explore the National Jazz Archive and search for interviews with female musicians. You will find very few. Look at venue rosters and festival programmes and see the paucity of women. Half the population, it seems, is virtually invisible in the UK jazz scene.

Speak to musicians in the UK and sooner or later, the lack of women playing jazz or attending jazz concerts will come up.

When "Women in Jazz" was published, I was astounded at the positive response it received. It was awarded a Jazz Times Distaff Award and made their Gearbox recommendation list. It was featured by the BBC as part of their International Women's Day programmes, had podcasts and videos made around it and was shortlisted for the Association of Jazz Journalists' Jazz Book of The Year. In the book, I interviewed 34 women of different ages, from different countries, and covered many issues. The interviews were informal and conversational. A perennial subject was the scarcity of fellow female jazz musicians, which the interviewees found most concerning.

This book looks at women in UK jazz and sees how the many initiatives and progressive ideas which have been implemented have impacted women who are performing today. Are there really many more men than women or are we just not seeing the women? If there are fewer female musicians, does it matter? How can the situation be changed? What is the way forward?

It offers a wide variety of perspectives on the issue along with the experiences of those in the industry, impressions from jazz lovers and other input that suggests the shortage of women in jazz is real. It then examines some of the reasons why and offers a few ways in which the situation can be remedied.

After a brief background to give the music context and of the history of women in UK jazz, this book investigates the premise of women in UK jazz in both a quantitative and qualitative sense. It looks at the numbers of women and men in festival line-ups, higher education, those attending jam sessions and those who gain employment in the industry as well as the gender pay gap. Other information is provided by venue managers, educators and musicians. In each area, contributions are made by those who have researched these areas.

To get some context of jazz's position as a genre and the UK as part of a worldwide industry, some references to other genres and countries are included. Jazz is a collaborative genre, mixing ages, genders and cultures probably more than any other music. It is multi-racial, multi-generational and made up of ensembles who may be an entity for just an evening, a tour or many years. It's music played by ensembles or adventurous soloists who come together from across the globe. Therefore, UK jazz cannot be unaffected by other scenes. There is also a lack of research available to those specifically investigating UK jazz. However, whilst it is useful to understand the situation in other countries, this book concentrates on the situation for women in UK jazz, and for UK academics, teachers, authors and venue managers.

Comprehending the situation and the possible reasons behind it helps us to see what still needs to be done to progress and bring UK jazz into the 21st century.

It is true that there are ongoing studies into gender issues in UK jazz and these are providing pointers as to how progress might be accelerated. Over the past few years, there has been a noticeable increase in support for female musicians and this comes from both men and women, yet talking to musicians themselves gives an insight into how far the research, discussions, panels, committees and initiatives have served to improve the visibility of female musicians in UK jazz.

This book seeks to understand the reasons for the continuing shortage of women in UK jazz. Female musicians and many others working in jazz give their perspectives and offer their experiences, whether they have experienced discrimination or not. The LGBTQ musicians and handful of male musicians mentioned here explain their understanding of the current situation and share their thoughts.

Finally, the book discusses whether there are potential problems with suddenly forcing gender parity; organisations which support the increase of visibility of female musicians in UK jazz; and approaches that could potentially fix the uneven playing field before looking towards the future.

Discussion is one thing. Creating lasting change is another. Until we have a true picture of the situation, how can we change it? Where is our starting point? If the numbers of women in jazz are low, where do we get more? Can we expect parity any time soon?

The majority of musicians understand that change needs to happen – both to enrich jazz music further and engage modern audiences. Female performers bring additional talent to the music and easily match the men in technical ability and improvisational skills. Yet the question remains. Where are they?

It must be remembered that progress has been made and there are initiatives which seek to raise not only the visibility of women in UK jazz but the importance of their music too. Many men consider females in their groups and many women and men work together on an equal basis but there is still work to be done.

Chapter 1

Background

From Jass into Jazz

In her book "Being Here"[1] author Radhika Philip writes, "The music was beautiful and effortlessly brought together strangely familiar sounds; sounds from different times and places which before that moment I could not have imagined hearing together".

Barack Obama once called jazz "the music of black working-class – largely invisible to the mainstream…. It went on to become America's most significant artistic contribution to the world". Miles Davis said, "Jazz is the big brother of revolution. Revolution follows it around". They were right. Jazz amalgamates the music of different cultures and because of the varied elements that it holds it connects us to the past and also reflects society in its changes and sub-genres. It was adopted officially by Congress as America's "national music" – even being protected by legislation: The National Jazz Preservation, Education, and Promulgation Act of 2017[2].

Jazz began in New Orleans around the turn of the 1900s. New Orleans was a centre for trade of many commodities – including slaves. Tribal rhythms, vocal hollers, songs,

---

[1] Philip, Radhika. "Being Here: Conversations on Creating Music", ISBN 978–0–9894880–0–6. Publisher: Radhio.org https://www.amazon.com/Radhio–org–Being–Here/dp/0615582222

[2] The National Jazz Preservation, Education and Promulgation Act of 2017 https://www.congress.gov/bill/115th–congress/house–bill/4626?s=1&r=10

dances and music styles were shared and elements of different cultures melded together. The elements of these different influences served as jazz's building blocks while the spirit of those who created it provided the alchemy needed to fuse them to create unique-sounding music.

"Jass" music (as it was first called) exploded when the putrid boil of resentment and oppression finally burst after being squeezed ever harder by the slave masters who'd captured and forcibly removed people from the lands of their birth. The music which took form in Congo Square and other places where slaves and free people could gather on Sundays and holidays expressed the spirits of the oppressed and those yearning for freedom.

The hollers and dance rhythms were honed and changed as rhythms from other lands were absorbed and instruments were swapped with free men who came to observe. Until 1871 when the mayor banned such gatherings, New Orleans was the seedbed from which grew an innovative and shockingly wonderful mix of musical styles which distilled eventually into "jass". It remained associated with New Orleans and the surrounding areas until it spread throughout America, aided immensely by the riverboats which networked the Mississippi and its tributaries, taking with them bands which played the music of Bolden, Morton and other luminaries. Each major city that the music reached added its cultural influences and jass continued to spread.

The power of *jass* attracted those who saw its commercial value and, like many good things, it was taken and turned into something sellable. Its new moniker, *jazz*, came into being because the rapacious men who controlled the commercial side of music felt it was a more appealing name. Whilst to some extent the Italian musicians who populated the river boat bands broke the strict race barriers, record companies found ways to segregate their customers by creating 'race' labels which sold one type of jazz music to part of the population whilst other commercial operations concentrated on propelling different artists to stardom on an international level. In many cases, record label managers – the "gatekeepers", as Adam Seiff, former head of jazz and blues at Sony, explained – grabbed control of all aspects of the music. Musicians were taken on by labels and shown to the public after careful grooming and marketing. Limited numbers of recordings were issued to keep the public thirsty for more, the distribution remaining in the hands of these gatekeepers.

Jazz was exported as a treasure from America, a gift to the world from Uncle Sam. When accusations of racism were levelled at the American government, particularly by the Soviet Union, black jazz musicians were sent worldwide as 'jazz ambassadors' to show the world how equality provided opportunities for everyone in the promised land. Jazz music's reward was protection by the aforementioned act of Congress.

New Orleans still bears the legacy of the creators of jazz: the exploited slaves and poor people of the city, the dispossessed given Sundays off by their God-fearing owners. You can still see, as I found when I visited last year, the huge houses of the Garden District there, once owned by slave masters, with their attached tiny properties where the slaves of the household would live. Still, the money in the city is largely visible in the rich suburbs where sprawling houses are fronted by well-maintained streets whilst just a few blocks away in poorer areas, damage from Hurricane Katrina from 2005 remains unrepaired.

By the time jazz reached New York, Chicago and other metropolises in America, the labels – and venues – were in control. Largely run by men, the venues were the dives, clubs and eateries where musicians played to customers for a fee or tips. In smaller clubs, singers would play the piano and sing for money given by those at the tables. The bigger your tips, and the more customers spent, the more likely you would stay in work. The nightclubs and venues in downtown New York and other cities where jazz bands played were not seen as places for 'decent women' because of their association with alcohol and drugs, both of which flowed freely.

To gain a place in a jazz band, cutting sessions became popular, where musicians turned up to a verbal invitation put out via the social networks of the time. Players would step up to play and see who could last the pace. They were brutal marathons and, whilst they were places for young musicians to hone their skills, there was a hierarchy and always the chance that someone better was waiting in the wings. The physically demanding sessions served to reinforce the male dominance of the club bands, though some exceptional women stood their ground as well as any man.

As it reached different countries, jazz absorbed aspects of the local culture and, though the intrinsic elements persisted, the music was subtly altered wherever it was played. It is still evolving: this is its very nature, as it is the music of reflection and expression. In the notes of a jazz standard, you can hear the oppression of the past, the joy of the moment and the hope for the future.

Right from the start of jazz there were women, of course – Billie Holiday, Ella Fitzgerald, Etta James, Sweet Emma Barrett, Nina Simone, Hazel Scott, Bessie Smith – the list of female performers is long, and women always had a place as supporters of musicians through managing their PR, arranging concerts, working out transport and so much more. Yet the jazz scene remained a male-dominated one. Women as bandleaders were very rare although there were exceptions. Sweet Emma Barrett, for example, had a lot going against her. She was 64 by the time she had her first successful recording, she was black, female and led an all-male band, the Preservation Hall Band of New Orleans. She endured mockery and proved her disparagers wrong by being one of the best pianists and improvisers New Orleans has ever known. She was also sassy, quirky and a character who carried her savings in her purse and travelled by train because she hated flying, with a hatbox full of food for the journey and always had a riposte – savoury or unsavoury – for those who questioned her ability (so not so sweet, after all). She was a rarity, though, and when jazz came to Europe and the UK the historically male-dominated scene prevailed.

There is an irony. The music which was hijacked and made money for the slick entrepreneurs of America was exported to all parts of the globe but it originated largely from imported rhythms, mostly from Africa, a continent which, at the time of jazz's emergence, couldn't have seemed more foreign to most Americans. These commercial men in suits were unwittingly adopting and protecting as their own music which, in its original forms, would have been as un-American as it is possible to be.

Jazz came about because of the tremendous suffering of people snatched from the country of their birth and enslaved in a foreign land, stripped of all rights and freedoms – apart, that is, from their music.

When jazz reached the UK, women somehow found themselves on the peripheries of the scene. Historical male dominance came with the imported music. Bottle clubs – the illegal drinking dens of the 1950s when austerity ruled in the UK post World War II; where the likes of George Melly, Humphrey Lyttleton, Ronnie Scott and Chris Barber played their music – were not welcoming to women, although they were asked there to dance. In the 1950s, there were even signs at some clubs stating "no jiving". This was austerity Britain. Jazz, in general, was played in smaller venues which were not considered respectful, so few women attended. It was rare to see a woman soloist or bandleader in the UK. Instead, the UK scene in its early days perpetuated the male-dominated aspects from across the pond. For some of the 1940s and 1950s, due in no small part to a disagreement between the musicians' unions of the US and the UK, few American musicians played in the UK and vice versa, limiting the exchange of styles which had happened before, so jazz in the UK diverged in style from the US and developed its own distinctive character before trans-Atlantic relations were restored.

Chapter 2

Women in UK Jazz, a Brief History

There have been books and studies which put the UK scene into historical context. Those including sections which highlight female musicians are rare and those which are entirely about UK female musicians rarer still.

In the late nineteenth and early twentieth century, women were largely involved in music as teachers. They were excluded both from orchestral and church music, yet many women were studying music at conservatoires. Having talent and being unable to use it except in a tutoring capacity led women to form small, women-only orchestras, chamber music groups and popular groups which played in coffee shops, restaurants and department stores.

Jazz had seeped into UK culture because of the popularity of music from America but was a dance style rather than music at first. After the First World War, women were enjoying freedom which came from supporting the industries whilst the men were away fighting. They had also enjoyed more in the way of sexual freedom and gained the right to vote. Jazz came along at just the right time to act as a backing track to the beginnings of emancipation of women in the UK. It became linked with women's freedom movements and a relaxation in societal expectations. For a while 'jazzing' was used to describe a freer set of sexual morals than would usually be expected of respectable young women in the early 1900s –

a term first used in New Orleans which those critical of the music gleefully gave to UK jazz.

This changed when outfits like the Original Dixieland Jazz Band came to London in 1919 and jazz as a genre grew in popularity. US stars came to the UK and women saw other women, usually as vocalists and pianists, perform this wonderful and slightly louche music which went against the conformity of post-war Britain. Female musicians played in jazz and dance bands, and some of the bands were mixed, a few all-female. By 1926, women were active in the UK jazz scene with female leaders including Blanche Coleman and Dorothy Marno. Women were also featured as soloists in male-led bands such as those of Teddy Joyce and Rudy Starita.

However, whilst the music may have been freer and less straitlaced, the critics were not. Many reviews focused not on the women's musical ability but on their looks and dress. Women were paid less than men and the Musicians' Union rarely supported women.

A few women formed all-female big bands. One of these was Ivy Benson who was born in Yorkshire in 1913. Benson was a cornerstone of change in the UK and through her all-female groups, many women found the confidence to form bands of their own. Performing since she was very young, Benson appeared on the BBC aged just nine years old and was nicknamed Baby Benson. She was a multi-instrumentalist, encouraged by her father, a musician himself who played in the Leeds Symphony Orchestra and other ensembles. Although her father wanted Benson to take the classical route, he did not stand in her way when she showed a love of popular music and began playing in

Edna Croudson's Rhythm Girls sextet. She played with them for almost six years part-time before joining Teddy Joyce's band and touring. She then moved to London and formed her own band, The Ivy Benson Rhythm Girls, after being encouraged by bandleader and composer Jack Hylton. The fact Benson had connections with the brass bands of the north of England, as well as popular ensembles, provided her with a pool of talented women to choose from.

In 1943 Benson and her band took a 22-week residency at the London Palladium before becoming a BBC House Band in Bristol. This booking was an affront to some male musicians and a delegation from the Musicians' Union met with the BBC to register their displeasure. Male bandleaders, apart from the ever-supportive Jack Hylton and British dance bandleader Joe Loss, resented Benson and her musicians. The critics were acerbic. During WWII, Benson's ensembles played at military bases which proved a strategic move, and they remained popular players of nostalgic and traditional numbers. Benson and her Rhythm Girls once again appeared at the Palladium and the Stoll Theatre (originally the London Opera House) in 1944. In 1945, Benson's authority as a bandleader was perhaps publicly validated when Field Marshall Montgomery asked her and her band to play at the VE Day celebrations in Berlin.

In 1946, fed up with the resentment over their success, Benson took her band on a European tour with ENSA (Entertainments National Service Association). Several trips to Europe and the Middle East followed. Her band remained popular into the 1980s. In an ironic twist, despite experiencing sexism, Benson had to change the name of the band to Ivy Benson and Her Showband because of the 1975 Sex Discrimination Act which made discrimination against women or men illegal in the workplace.

Without strong leaders like Benson, who seemed to be able to navigate the overt sexism in the UK in the early to mid-twentieth century, many women would not have had the opportunity to play alongside quality female musicians. Benson and her bands were known for playing nostalgic music but several musicians who cut their teeth in her bands left and played more diverse, modern jazz, picking up on the changing rhythms seeping into the UK from abroad. Several of these had long-lasting careers of their own.

One of the musicians who started as a member of Benson's band is drummer Crissy Lee, who left Benson's band in the late 1960s to form her own band, The Beat Chicks. Later in the 1990s, her jazz orchestra became popular, and Crissy launched her own jazz club which is still going strong. She found being a female drummer brought its own problems. On one occasion, four members of an orchestra left when they heard the guest drummer was to be a woman. Many times, when Lee turned up with her sticks in a bag, people would ask if she was carrying them for her brother or dad. However, Crissy, as one of the UK's best jazz drummers, took little more than the opening bars of the first number to silence any doubters.

Trombonist Annie Whitehead had a successful career within all-female and mixed-gender groups and as a session musician since leaving Benson's band in the 1970s. She led and wrote for her own bands in the 1980s and in 2002 she formed the all-female Vortex Foundation Big Band.

Other important women in UK jazz had their original break in Ivy Benson's bands. These include trumpet player Gracie Cole and saxophone players and composers Barbara Thompson and Gail Thompson (no relation).

Deirdre Cartwright bought her first electric guitar in 1971 and began to teach herself to play, keeping her wish to play in a band a secret from the nuns at her convent school. By the time she was 17 she had discovered blues and jazz and was playing in a number of bands. In 1976 she joined Jam Today which introduced her to the London left-wing feminist lesbian movement whilst she was also playing in the heavy rock band Painted Lady who later had worldwide hits as Girlschool.

In 1970s Britain, many female musicians played together at gigs, parties, benefits, major political conferences and women-only events. Jam Today set up their own feminist record label, Stroppy Cow, and members of the band, who included bass player Alison Rayner, were active in constructing support networks for female musicians. Cartwright was part of curating women-only jam sessions where they could learn from each other and here she met pianist Laka Daisical and saxophonist Ruthie Smith. Deirdre formed the pop band Tour de Force in 1979 with her sister Bernice and they signed to EMI.

Cartwright's love of jazz led her to join the nascent band The Guest Stars in 1981. Formed by Ruthie Smith, their mix of Afrobeat, jazz and Latin led them to become a highly influential group during the 1980s, recording several albums and touring extensively. Two larger groups with the

Guest Stars at their core were the Lydia D'Ustebyn Swing Orchestra and the Sisterhood of Spit. In 1983, whilst busking in Covent Garden with two other Guest Star band members, BBC producer Chris Lent spotted her and offered her the role of guitar presenter on the BBC show Rockschool. This was introduced by Herbie Hancock from the US.

Other important influencers included Deirdre Cartwright. In 1991 she formed her own band, the Deirdre Cartwright Group, which has toured widely and played numerous festivals. Members of the Guest Stars went their separate ways but re-formed briefly in 2004. The long-term musical partnership between Cartwright and Alison Rayner led to the organisation Blow the Fuse (more later) as well as other projects, including ARQ, Rayner's Parliamentary Award winning quintet.

A group which inspired many female free-jazz players was the Feminist Improvising Group (FIG) which formed in 1977 and, as the name suggests, was overtly supportive of women's rights. There was already an interest in anarchic improvisational music, largely as a result of the changing political climate in the 1960s, which had originated in Europe and come across to the UK. This movement encouraged musicians to experiment and kick back against the expected conformity of the day. Peter Brötzmann, a notable veteran of free jazz, recently explained in a conversation that the movement was a reaction by young people to mistakes made by politicians and to the race riots in the US, the student revolutions and the falling of barriers across the world in terms of social and political norms.

FIG was ground-breaking because the free improvisation movement had largely been expressed by male, white musicians like Brötzmann in Europe and Evan Parker in the UK. These women challenged the ownership of freely improvised music by men. FIG included vocalist Maggie Nicols and multi-instrumentalist and composer Lindsay Cooper who saw that women were being excluded. The playing of improvised music by women in the UK is still linked to women's rights and political issues in the minds of some. Critics of the women who performed improvised music early on – often with art and visual concepts presented to the audience alongside the music – called into question their technical abilities and complained about the lack of men in their ranks, which is odd because no one questioned the lack of women in most jazz groups.

Over the course of its development into one of the world's premier jazz scenes, UK jazz has produced stellar female performers including vocalists Cleo Laine, Norma Winstone, Anita Wardell, Liane Carroll, Deelee Dubé and Julie Dexter, pianists Natalie Spencer and Nikki Iles, pianist and vocalist Marian McPartland, 'cello player Shirley Smart, trombone player Sarah Gail Brand, drummer Sophie Alloway, saxophonist Trish Clowes...the list is long and these are just a few of the influential and important women of the UK scene.

So, given their numbers and their historical influence on the UK jazz scene, why are women not more visible? Where are their photographs, their interviews, articles, reviews and everything else we might expect? Why does the National Jazz Archive[3] hold pictures mainly of men? Why can most people name male musicians and not female ones? Search the National Jazz Archive interviews and you will have to look hard to find any women interviewed. You will eventually find Crissy Lee, Sue Robinson, Elaine Delmar, Norma Winstone and Susan May, and a few women are mentioned in journals and articles. Yet there are very few UK women highlighted to the extent men are, which is a shame. Where are they? Where are Alison Affleck, Jo Harrop, Georgia Mancio, Emily Saunders, Faye Patton, Emma Fisk, Sue Richardson, Yazz Ahmed, Helen Papaioannou, Zoe Gilby? This is our nation's jazz archive: surely it should contain more females given the many already mentioned here, and we have hardly even started.

Don't misunderstand, the National Jazz Archive (NJA) is a wonderful collection of photographs, documents and records of those who came to the UK and those who helped shape the jazz here. It's fascinating to lose yourself amongst the archives and sense the wonder of the music, but the lack of females is striking and disproportionate to the actual number of women who have been part of UK jazz for decades. For this book, the NJA offered the use of a photograph of a female UK jazz musician from its archive collections by two photographers. Surprisingly, there were none to be found in either collection. It is not the NJA's fault, though. The media seem to have airbrushed women out, erased their presence in UK jazz. More recently, several magazines have run feature articles on the rising

---

[3] National Jazz Archive https://nationaljazzarchive.org.uk/ Loughton Library, Traps Hill, Loughton,Essex IG10 1HD

female UK jazz musicians but they should be documented more, highlighted and included just like the men. Sadly, still, they are not.

Alison Rayner © Jane C. Reid

Alison Affleck © Colin Black

Helen Papaioannou © Phil Barnes

Zoe Gilby © Malcolm Sinclair

Emma Fisk © Malcolm Sinclair

Jo Harrop © Malcolm Sinclair

Norma Winstone © Colin Black

Chapter 3

The UK: Facts and Observations

Whilst seeking an understanding of the lack of women in jazz in the UK, there are some possible explanations. Could it be, for example, that women simply don't like jazz? Do men and women hear music differently? US author Walter Kolosky ("Power, Passion and Beauty"[4]) says, "Are fewer women than men, musician or not, drawn to jazz because they hear it differently? I think so. Though jazz is a high art, there also seems to be something very primal, and male, in real jazz music". Could this be true? Or do fewer women play jazz because teachers and parents don't encourage girls to pick up instruments which can be played in jazz ensembles or bands?

Are men unable to cope with women playing on an equal platform? Are women chosen for their looks and not their talent? Are women intimidated because of the lack of female role models or mentors? Do women adapt less well to late nights and touring? Do women just want to have kids, stay at home and be supported by their partners?

Is the lack of women in jazz still even true? Have we just become so used to saying it, like a mantra? I can think of great male jazz performers and also great female ones, so why is the talk still about the shortage of women?

---

[4] Kolosky, Walter. "Power, Passion Beauty", ISBN–10: 0976101629. Publisher: Abstract Logix.

There are so many questions and most of us could hazard a guess at the answers, but guessing is not enough. We need to understand. There are many great jazz men and women but most of the women are vocalists and pianists and mostly, they are not from the UK.

To put the situation into context, women are lacking in jazz, not just in the UK but everywhere, and whilst the lack of visibility is a problem here, the UK is not alone. Across the pond in America, if you look through the list of interviewees in the DownBeat Book of Great Jazz Interviews published in 2009 celebrating 75 years of publication, there is an astounding lack of female presence. Even the great female stars of the US are not there. Each section has articles from a particular decade. From the 1930s there are 12 articles, none of which are about a woman. From the 1940s there are12 articles, and only one (8.33%) is about a woman. From the 1950s there are 19 articles with two (10.53%) about women. The 1960s has 25 articles and, again two (8%) are about women. In the 1970s there are 16 articles with none featuring women. Only one of the 15 articles from the 1980s (6.66%) is about a woman. The 1990s has two out of 18 articles (11.11%) and in the 2000s there are 12 articles and none are about women. Considering these are DownBeat's "Great Jazz Interviews" is it surprising out of a total of 129 articles just eight are about women (6.20%), although a few get a mention in some of the articles about men? The representation of women falls way below their actual presence in the US jazz scene.

Biddy Healey's 2016 blog article "Be a Good Girl or Play Like a Man: Why Women Aren't Getting into Jazz"[5] was written as part of a university assignment. Healey put her findings in the blog post, and these have become much-cited by those seeking to understand gender disparity. Although the work was carried out at an Australian university where Healey was enrolled in a highly respected jazz course, many of her findings resonate with the UK situation, namely that out of 40 students enrolled in a jazz course at a top-flight Australian university, only 12 (30%) were women. Of these, six were vocalists, one a drummer, one a sax player and two were pianists. Two subsequently dropped out, leaving 10 women (25%) in the course. Therefore, it is not a UK specialism but something which is true in other countries too. There was a very low number of female students compared to males which made Healey question why women weren't getting in or if they were even applying.

When she surveyed colleges, she found it was not a case of women not passing auditions. They simply were not applying in the first place. The underrepresentation of women began well before anyone signed up for auditions – in jazz courses, anyway.

She asked her tutor why he thought more women weren't coming into jazz. He replied it was "a 'blokey' art form".

Other responses told her that the qualities needed to get ahead in jazz were held to be 'masculine'; women have a

---

[5] Healey, Biddy. "Be a Good Girl and Play Like a Man" (2016).
http://www.biddyhealey.com/blog/2016/6/18/be–a–good–girl–or–play–like–a–man

fear of looking unattractive whilst playing, and a desire for marriage betrayed a lack of 'male' ambition. Healey's title for her blog piece incidentally comes from a book by Lewis A. Erenberg called "Swingin' The Dream"[6] where he quotes a 1940s DownBeat piece in which the author advises that women could either be "good girls" or "play like men". The former forced them to emphasise looks over musical ability; the latter used their unexpected musical talent to nullify their sexuality.

Other findings in Healey's research which resonate in the UK were that many women felt socially excluded in male-dominated ensembles. Jazz is a social art because it is freelance and ensemble-based. Women reported being excluded from banter and not invited to post-gig discussions or drinks.

The idea of enforcing parity has been mooted by various initiatives and studies but with this idea comes potential problems.

If quotas are imposed, making it binding that festivals include more women, could this lead to an inherent bias against men? Equally, could women feel they might lose out because a venue has met its female "quota"? It's important to select musicians on ability alone. With a small pool of female musicians, the likelihood of a female being selected in the first place is reduced. However, for a male bandleader, it can be tricky because if he feels he should select a female musician but none of the women he knows plays the style he wants, he is in danger of losing the sound

---

[6] Erenberg, Lewis A. "Swingin' the Dream: Big Band Jazz and the Rebirth of American Culture", Chicago: University of Chicago Press, 1999, ISBN 9780226215174. Publisher: University of Chicago Press.

he seeks. If he can find no suitable females and selects a man, he is in danger of being labelled sexist. If, as some would like to see, quotas are introduced to dictate the numbers of men or women who can play, how is this supporting free choice of musicians, male or female? Could that encourage tokenism? Is it right to put a formula on an art form? This confusing scenario needs clarification.

There have been studies into gender in jazz music. Selections which make intriguing reading are listed at the end of this book. However, these capture a fleeting moment and are limited in their findings to the criteria set, so the task is how to find out what is happening right now.

Festivals

Festivals are a big part of the UK music industry and there is typically a crop of annual events at the local and national level, several of which specialise in jazz. They vary in size, some having a large number of acts over several days of events, whilst others have fewer acts and take place over a weekend or just one or two days.

Jazz music is also included in festivals covering a wider spectrum, such as Maverick Festival UK which bills itself as an Americana event and "a beacon of roots music from both sides of the Atlantic". It includes over 50 acts of jazz, blues and country music. Other annual festivals like Snape Proms, Glastonbury, Latitude and Bath Festival are just a few which incorporate jazz into their programmes.

A look through jazz festival programmes gives an overview of the number of acts engaged to perform and the number of acts which are female or where the bandleader is billed as female. The highly respected Sandy Brown list of jazz festivals[7] includes major festivals in the UK. Recent additions not yet on the list are Southend Jazz Festival and Walthamstow Jazz Festival, both of which began in 2019.

The quality of acts at UK jazz festivals is indicative of the respect with which the UK is viewed. International stars come and play, and these have included Pharoah Sanders, Dwight Trible, Grace Jones, Gladys Knight, Snarky Puppy as well as popular home-grown UK jazz performers such as Jamie Cullum, Courtney Pine, Kit Downes, GoGo Penguin, Jools Holland, Sarah Tandy, The Pasadena Roof Orchestra and many more. The festivals also serve to introduce popular local bands to a wider audience. Who knew there were bands called Frog & Henry and the Jelly Roll Quartet? At a festival, guests can see a range of genres and styles, big and small bands, and solo artists. Around any festival are associated businesses and events including readings, poetry, book sales, CD sales, and food and drink events so these events have important social, economic and networking benefits. Large numbers of people attend UK jazz festivals. According to David Jones of Serious (an organization which curates the London Jazz Festival), the London Jazz Festival has been getting in excess of 100,000 people attending each year.

To see if there was a difference between the number of male and female acts, statistics on festival line-ups were obtained for the past two to four years. The billings were checked and the number of male and female soloists and male- and female-led bands recorded. Also recorded was

---

[7] Sandy Brown List, UK Jazz Festivals
https://www.sandybrownjazz.co.uk/Features/UKJazzFestivals2019.html

the number of mixed bands because these would contain female members, to see whether including these would raise the percentage of acts including females. The charts which follow show the number of male, female and mixed acts performing at each festival. Where the billing was unclear on the gender of an act, posters were checked to see if a band was male, female or mixed. Bands could not be included where the gender of members was unclear from the name and there was no poster to clarify. "Male" means bands billed under the name of a male leader or where a solo act is male, and "female" is where a band is billed as led by a female performer or where the solo act is female. "Mixed" has both male and female leads or it means the band is mixed. The percentage of male, female and mixed performers is at the bottom of the chart for each festival.

Fig. 1. Numbers of male, female and mixed acts, Edinburgh Jazz and Blues Festival

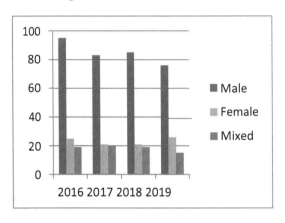

Percentage of female performers, Edinburgh Jazz and Blues Festival

2016	2017	2018	2019
17.98	16.93	18.26	22.22

Percentage female plus mixed acts, Edinburgh Jazz and Blues Festival

2016	2017	2018	2019
31. 65	33.1	32	37.22

Fig. 2. Numbers of male, female and mixed acts, Herts Jazz Festival

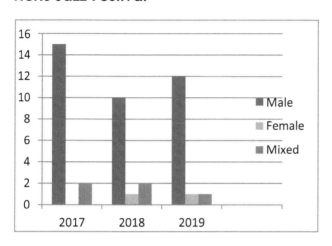

Percentage female performers, Herts Jazz Festival

2017	2018	2019
0.00	7.69	7.14

Percentage female and mixed acts, Herts Jazz Festival

2017	2018	2019
0.00	30	16.66

Fig. 3. Numbers of male, female and mixed acts, Swanage Jazz Festival

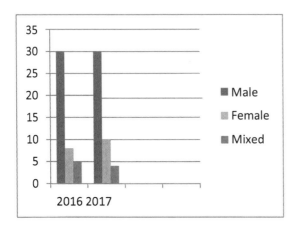

Percentage female performers, Swanage Jazz Festival
2016   2017
18.6   22.73

Percentage female and mixed acts, Swanage Jazz Festival
2016   2017
43.33   31.81

Fig. 4. Numbers of male, female and mixed acts, Pershore Jazz Festival

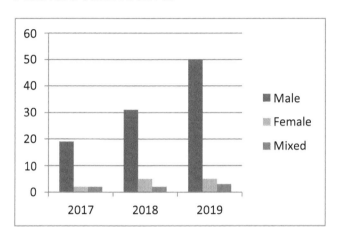

Percentage female performers, Pershore Jazz Festival
2017   2018   2019
8.69   13.51   8.62

Percentage female and mixed acts, Pershore Jazz Festival
2017   2018   2019
17.39   18.42   13.79

Fig. 5. Numbers of male, female and mixed acts, Lancaster Jazz Festival

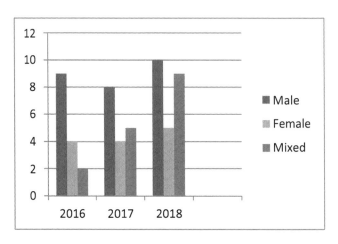

Percentage female performers, Lancaster Jazz Festival

2016	2017	2018
26.6	23.52	20.83

Percentage female and mixed acts, Lancaster Jazz Festival

2016	2017	2018
40	52.94	58.33

Fig. 6. Numbers of male, female and mixed acts, Love Supreme Festival (headline acts only; this festival is one of the largest)

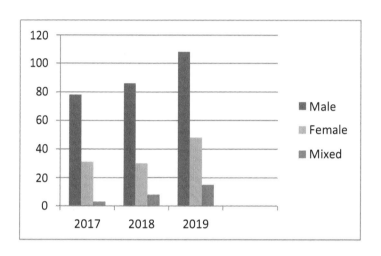

Percentage female performers, Love Supreme Festival

2017	2018	2019
27.67	24.19	28.07

Percentage female and mixed acts, Love Supreme Festival

2017	2018	2019
30.63	30.64	36.84

Fig. 7 Numbers of male, female and mixed acts, City of Derry Jazz and Big Band Festival

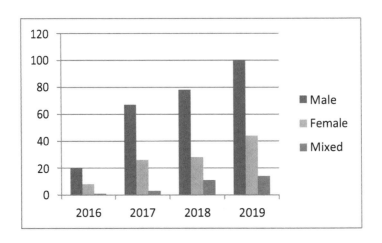

Percentage female musicians, City of Derry Jazz and Blues Festival

2016	2017	2018	2019
27.59	24.52	23.93	27.84

Percentage female and mixed acts, City of Derry Jazz and Blues Festival

2016	2017	2018	2019
33.33	30.20	33.33	36.7

Fig. 8 Numbers of male, female and mixed acts, Ribble Valley Jazz and Blues Festival

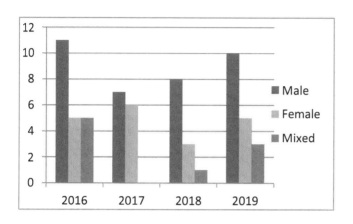

Percentage female performers, Ribble Valley Blues and Jazz Festival

2016	2017	2018	2019
23.80	46.15	25.00	27.77

Percentage female and mixed acts, Ribble Valley Blues and Jazz Festival

2016	2017	2018	2019
52.33	46.15	33.33	44.44

Fig. 9. Numbers of male, female and mixed acts, London Jazz Festival

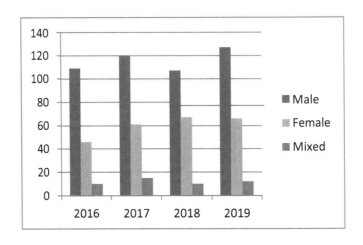

London Jazz Festival percentage women performers, London Jazz Festival

2016	2017	2018	2019
27.88	31.12	36.41	32.19

Percentage female and mixed acts, London Jazz Festival

2016	2017	2018	2019
33.93	38.77	41.84	38.04

Fig. 10. Numbers of male, female and mixed acts, 2020 line-ups (festivals cancelled due to COVID-19 but three formalised line-ups are included)

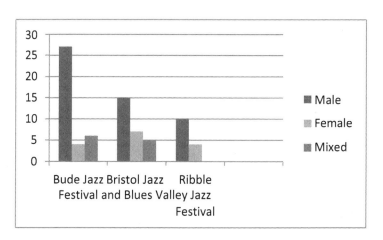

From the charts, it can be seen that the disparity between male and female-led acts is clear. In every case, the number of female performers is below 50% – often by a long way. By factoring in the mixed groups – which means there was at least one woman present on stage – the percentage rises considerably, with one or two (Lancaster 2017 and Ribble Valley 2016) even rising just above the 50% mark but for most, the increase only takes the share of female performers to around 33%. When a festival increased in size like Pershore, which went from 38 to 58 acts from 2018-2019, the increase in the number of women performers was not in line with the increase in the total number of acts, and in fact the percentages for female performers and mixed acts fell. In Derry, as the number of male acts rose in 2019 with an increase of 22 acts, the number of women-led acts also rose but at a lower rate than the rise for male acts with just 16 more. What is obvious is the number of female-led acts at festivals remains very small.

In 2017, the London Jazz Platform, a day festival, took place. Fourteen acts played across a day. A gentleman who had been there all day commented, "Well, I have never been to an event like this where there are so many women. It's overrun with 'em". As curator I had chosen the acts for their talent and had not given much thought to their gender. Female acts included Gg (Harold), Kitty LaRoar, Carmela Rappazzo and Sarah Gail Brand, and there were some women in groups, but out of a total of 41 musicians, just 10 were women. Why would this man feel 'overrun' when under 25% of the performers were female? It should be remembered this was just one man out of about 100 people who came to the event, and the majority of people there paid no heed to the gender of the performers; but the fact he even brought the subject up was surprising. Would an event comprising an all-male line-up generate a comment? Festivals are just part of the puzzle, however, and more data is needed.

The good news about festivals is that their organizers have been talking about disparity issues and thinking about ways to tackle them. The Teignmouth Jazz and Blues Festival identified three key areas where work was needed: the age range of their audiences, the dearth of attendees or musicians from the BAME (Black, Asian and Minority Ethnic) community, and the lack of female musicians.

Ian Roberts, Chair of the Teignmouth Jazz and Blues Festival, realized there was a burgeoning young jazz audience in the metropolitan areas which was not happening in the more provincial areas (Devon, SW England) so the festival invited bands from London to perform. They also worked with Jazz South to find bands they could showcase at the festival, and they actively sought out bands which included members of different cultures and ethnicities. They also sought to redress the balance in terms of male to female performers.

According to Roberts, "We were conscious that the huge majority of jazz (and blues) musicians were male – male, white, elderly actually – so we decided to make a big effort in 2019 to seek out female bands, female-led bands and musicians". In many bands with females they were the vocalists, but this festival also sought out bands with female musicians and solo acts. They succeeded; acts like saxophonist Roz Harding and others played, and the balance of male-to-female musicians rose from nearly zero to around 45%, a massive change for the festival.

"The effect on the festival's audiences over the weekend were very positive", Roberts said. "More females meant gigs were female-friendly, and we noticed more women coming on their own instead of as partners of performers, so it affected the dynamics in a very positive way".

The Teignmouth festival also introduced a series of incidental gigs titled "The Lady Sings" outside of the main festival events. They held a few before COVID stopped proceedings, and joined forces with a local theatre which meant they could afford to pay bigger fees to get high-flying female vocalists including Kyla Brox, Odette Adams and Gabrielle Ducomble.

Roberts added, "Female singers do attract men but they also attract other women who feel comfortable in the audience," so it becomes a win-win on both sides. For areas outside the main cities to get these major stars is also a real bonus for the events. The festival organises monthly club nights and recently the number of female-leading acts rose to almost 40%, which is an increase from 2017 when the acts were nearly all male. These events have a balance of singers and instrumentalists. Roberts and the rest of those running the Teignmouth Jazz and Blues Festival have made a targeted effort to increase their numbers of young people, those from the BAME community and women, and it works because their audiences are more diverse, young people feel more welcome, and women feel more comfortable in attending. This shows that attention to parity results in a positive outcome for events, not to mention very favourable kudos.

Education figures

According to the Higher Education Statistics Authority, out of 10,000 people studying all forms of music performance each year from 2013-18, between 100-150 studied jazz performance. In classical and popular music, women were more equally represented with gender being roughly balanced. Some jazz musicians came through having studied a non-specialist degree and some musicians of course find success without any formal study, but the figures of students studying at higher levels tell an interesting story. The chart below shows degrees with a jazz specialisation as reported to the Authority from 2013-18.

Fig. 11. Percentages of male and female students entering jazz performance studies at the tertiary level in the UK

Academic year	Level of study	Subject	Female %	Male %
2017/18	Postgraduate	Jazz Performance	18.18	81.82
	Undergraduate	Jazz Performance	11.69	88.31
2016/17	Postgraduate	Jazz Performance	0.00	100
	Undergraduate	Jazz Performance	9.09	90.91
2015/16	Postgraduate	Jazz Performance	0.00	100
	Undergraduate	Jazz Performance	25.30	74.70
2013/14	Postgraduate	Jazz Performance	21.46	78.54
	Undergraduate	Jazz Performance	12.50	87.50

When the figures are put into a chart (see Fig. 12), the differences are stark. (With thanks to Vick Bain for these figures.)

Fig. 12. Chart showing percentages of male to female students studying jazz performance in the UK from 2013-2018

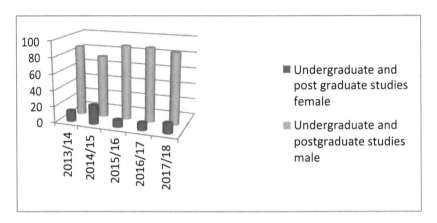

Interestingly, research by Vick Bain[8] found that from GCSE to A levels, the participation of males and females in music was roughly equal. Out of 25,900 students studying music-related subjects vs. all degree-related subjects, 44.33% were female in 2018 and of the 5,295 students studying music at post-graduate levels 49.40% were female. Other studies have found that in jazz orchestras and ensembles in schools, the ratio of males to females is roughly equal, with male students just slightly outnumbering females. So why, when it gets to the tertiary level, are so few women studying jazz? What is happening between secondary school and college or university?

---

[8] "Counting the Music Industry: The Gender Gap, A Study of Gender Inequality in the UK Music Industry". Report by Vick Bain. https://countingmusic.co.uk/
https://www.musicweek.com/publishing/read/a–wake–up–call–vick–bain–on–her–report–into–gender–inequality–in–music/077734

Could one of the reasons be a lack of role models and inspirational figures in colleges and conservatoires? When teaching staff at institutions offering jazz studies are researched, the male-to-female ratio of staff is overwhelmingly male. The examples below are from college websites.

Fig. 13. Chart showing numbers of male to female teaching staff in jazz courses in the UK, 2020

Institution	Male members of teaching staff	Female members of teaching staff
Leeds College of Music	27	3
Trinity Laban	30	4
Royal Academy of Music	51	3
Guildhall	105	12*

*Includes visiting artists

So, if you are female and going to view music colleges and considering jazz as an option, who is going to be your inspiration or who will you see in the positions of authority? Fellow women? Unlikely.

You may wonder why all this is important. Is jazz not a tiny part of a tiny industry? Why is music in the UK important at all? In the past, that would have been a difficult question to quantify. Collating all the tickets sold, concerts attended, live performances, prices paid and profits made would have been a massive task. Luckily there was an organisation willing to prove the value to the economy of music. UK Music is an industry-funded body, established in October 2008, to represent the collective interests of the recorded, published and live arms of the British music industry. In November 2019 they published an inaugural study called "Music by Numbers" which revealed that music contributes a staggering £5.2 billion to the UK economy and is growing. Jazz is a small but important part of that industry so it is important to many venues, ensures staff have jobs, generates income and attracts the young people who will be its future.

Papers

There have been several studies carried out by respected academics into UK music and gender in jazz music. For this book, research was shared by people whose studies hold pertinent information.

Vick Bain is a music industry consultant, researcher and campaigner. Bain also helped set up the Jazz Committee at the British Academy of Songwriters, Composers and Authors (BASCA) when she was the CEO and worked with several jazz composers over the years including Emily Saunders, who is very actively campaigning on behalf of women in jazz. Bain is also a PhD researcher of women in the music industry at Queen Mary University, amongst other roles.

Joy Ellis is a jazz pianist, composer, arranger, vocalist and Guildhall School of Music and Drama Master's graduate. She presented a paper written by herself and her husband, Adam Osmianski, who is a lecturer for West Virginia University, a percussionist and drummer.

Andrea Vicari is on the professorial staff at Trinity Laban Conservatoire of Music and Dance. She is also a bandleader and composer and directs and manages many summer school activities.

All of these individuals have produced key papers which have studied different aspects of the music industry in the UK and included jazz. There are other researchers who will be mentioned later.

In October 2019 Vick Bain carried out a study titled "Counting the Music Industry: The Gender Gap". This was a study of gender inequality in the UK music industry. It concentrated on the gender balance of those signed to publishers and labels because these are the careers which are nurtured and funded by the industry (as opposed to self-published or self-released music).

She found that of musicians signed to 106 music publishers, just over 14% were female, and of those signed to 219 record labels, 20% were female. Of those working for 126 UK music publishers, 36.67% were female. These figures cover all genres, not just jazz but they highlight the shortage of women signed to publishers or labels, and also raise the question of whether fewer women are signed to or work for music companies because there are so few women already there.

At the time of the study, most companies probably felt they had successfully navigated the tricky area of diversity and equality, but Bain's findings showed there was a long way to go when she looked at their staff (with just over one third being female) and signings. Then again with 82% of the CEOs of music publishers being male, is that such a surprise?

Bain's paper goes on to cite many examples of disparity between males and females in sectors like music commissions, awards, and the fact that at PRS for Music, the royalty collection organisation for songwriters and composers in the UK, just 17% of its 140,000 registered members are female (in 2018).

Pulling the figures for jazz from Bain's research and looking at jazz artists on rosters, the research shows just 10.87% were female which is even lower than for most festival line-ups. Jazz singers comprise a (comparatively) high number of solo artists at 26%, but the overall number is dramatically lowered by the low representation of women in groups at 8%. Jazz proved to have the largest disparity between male and female performers of all genres. Thus, it appears women are somehow excluded from jazz groups despite the increasingly larger number of women in the scene.

Why is this important? It is important because if fewer female musicians are signed to labels, fewer will have access to good promoters and be experienced enough to get major contracts like festival gigs. Unless more female musicians are signed, their numbers will remain lower at festivals and other performance types. Some festival organisers have stated that they want more women and some have been successful but it is a problem actually finding them. The pool is limited.

A year on from her research, Bain says, "Jazz was so interesting because it had the greatest discrepancy between the numbers of female solo artists and those in bands and was definitely in the lower end of genres for female inclusion on the labels. I believe this is indicative of a form of homophily, the desire for men to only want to play music with other men, which is particularly prevalent in jazz music culture. From my reading and conversations with female jazz musicians, I also believe the emphasis on competitive improvisation can be very disempowering for young female jazz musicians and put them off the genre. And the dominance of male professors at the universities too. So, complex reasons but the data is very stark".

In 2015 Joy Ellis produced a paper[9] with Adam Osmianski titled "Women and the Jazz Jam". It was presented as part of the 14th Darmstadt Jazzforum in Berlin which took as its title "XYXX Jazz" and looked into gender and identity in jazz.

In the paper, Ellis and Osmianski discuss the role of the jazz jam[10] as an element within jazz since its early days, and more so since the development of the bebop style of playing which concentrates more on individual rather than ensemble playing. The paper looks at many studies including those of William B. Cameron[11], Erin Wehr-Flowers[12] and others. The authors also discuss and draw

---

[9] "Women and the Jazz Jam" written for and presented at the 14th Darmstadt Jazzforum on Gender Identity in 2015 by Joy Ellis and Adam Osmianski. https://www.jazzinstitut.de/gender_identity_jazz/?lang=en

[10] Jam sessions are events where musicians join with others in spontaneous ensembles, or they are invited as part of the selection process. They are also sometimes held just for the enjoyment of playing together. They have, to a large extent, replaced cutting sessions of the past.

[11] Cameron, William Bruce. "Sociological Notes on the Jam Session", Social Forces Journal, Volume 33, Issue 2, December 1954, Pages 177-182. https://doi.org/10.2307/2573543

[12] Wehr–Flowers, Erin. "Differences between Male and Female Students' Confidence, Anxiety, and Attitude Toward Learning Jazz Improvisation", Journal of Research in Music Education 54, No. 4 (Winter, 2006): 337–349.

their own conclusions based on a broad and thorough array of observations, analyses and direct questioning of musicians, the majority of whom lived in Europe and North America and whose predominant experience was the UK and US jazz scenes. Across countries, Ellis and Osmianski found little variation in responses.

Before jazz degrees and jazz studies at conservatoires, musicians earned their reputations and demonstrated their skills by turning up and lasting (or not) the course of a jam session. Historically, reference to jam sessions used language such as a 'brotherhood', a 'fraternity of brothers' and 'battles of war' – all very masculine. Women seldom had a presence because the sessions were often held late at night, not accessible to women, and the qualities perceived as important to make one's way in the jazz world were aggression, power and self-confidence – ostensibly 'male' attributes.

Jam sessions today are not the be-all-and-end-all of a musician's progress and many find other ways of playing together, especially through opportunities provided in colleges. However, they are historically intrinsic to jazz and turning up at some jam sessions, as opposed to sitting in (where particular musicians are invited to play with a band), is still seen as something of a tradition. Others view them as trial by peers.

The facts in the paper were gleaned from interviews with jazz musicians. They were asked their age, sex, country, whether they attended jam sessions and if these resulted in unpaid or paid work. They were also asked about how active they were in their jazz community and

how much of their income came from playing jazz. Of the
187 respondents, 64 were women and 123 men.

Fig. 14. Responses to statements provided by Ellis and Osmianski

Statement/Questions	% Men who agree	% Women who agree
I find it easy to sit in and play at a jam session	54	25
I have been treated differently when I sat in and played at a jam session as a result of my gender	5	44
Attended more than 50 jam sessions	65	53
Played at more than 50 jam sessions	58	33
Received paid work as a direct result of a jam session	68	34

These are only some of the findings of the paper (which
is recommended reading) but a few things become
apparent.

Firstly, twice the percentage of men found it easy to sit
in and play at a jam session. A large percentage of women
compared to men felt they were treated differently due to

their gender. Also, twice the percentage of men received paid employment as a result of jam sessions. An interesting other fact which Ellis and Osmianski found was 22% of men said they felt uncomfortable in jam sessions because they could be intimidating and several said it depended on who was running it.

Why jam sessions still take place when there are other ways of hearing different artists' music is another interesting question. You can hear CDs and online sessions, for example. Part of the answer is undoubtedly that jam sessions remain a key social networking time for musicians. They also carry on traditions which preserve the history of jazz playing. Jam sessions rely heavily on improvisation skills which both women and men have in equal measure but they also depend upon the connectivity between musicians. With fewer women attending or feeling comfortable, it could be women are denied the possibilities of forming the musical connections their male counterparts enjoy.

One of the key characteristics of jazz music is expression. The music allows inner feelings and thoughts to emerge, develop and be shared. Is jazz music itself perhaps a key to unlocking gender parity? This expressive music, so loved and cherished by a core of people, could be the music which leads. Improvisation is individual so your level of comfort and background is obviously going to have an effect on the sound you play. Musicians who feel support will reward the audience and fellow band members with music which sings from the heart, unfettered by distractive thoughts like 'should I be here?' or 'am I good enough?'

Several commentators note the lack of female role models in running jam sessions, so perhaps more established female musicians hosting jam sessions would improve the confidence of women to attend and participate.

Women attending a jam session probably feel a bit like a man attending a mother and toddler group. He will be made welcome, he might see another dad, but there will be areas he feels uncomfortable and shut out of.

Andrea Vicari's paper[13] on those studying instrumental jazz in higher education was undertaken to discover whether the numbers of women were low in comparison to men. By looking at various institutions to discover how many women are currently studying jazz, which instruments they play and numbers of women auditioning, some conclusions were made. Data was gathered from a survey, which asked questions of leading jazz musicians involved in jazz education, such as: 1) Where do you teach? 2) How many jazz students are in your department? 3) How many women students are in the jazz department? 4) What instruments do the women play? 5) Do you participate in the audition process for your college? 6) What is the gender balance in jazz auditions? 7) Do you have any methods for actively recruiting women? 8) Do you feel there is a need to actively recruit women for jazz courses? Respondents were also asked to confirm their institution details and whether they had anything to add.

Vicari's paper is particularly interesting because it concentrates mainly on UK institutions, though it includes some data from institutions in other countries. As part of

---

[13] Vicari, Andrea. "Gender Imbalance in the Number of Women Studying Instrumental Jazz at Higher Education Level" http://www.andreavicari.com/newpages/trypmenu.html

her research, a questionnaire was sent out to schools, regional jazz orchestras, HE colleges, summer schools and conservatoires. Seventy-one percent of the schools said that between 50-72% of students receiving instrumental lessons were female and between 50-80% of participants in jazz activities were male. The average gender divide in the regional jazz ensembles was 60% male, 40% female and across the seven summer schools it was 81% male, 19% female. So already we can see 21% fewer girls audition for summer school than play jazz in school.

A question might be if 50-80% of the participants in jazz activities in school were male and so 20-50% female (depending on activity), why are there not 20-50% females auditioning for jazz summer schools? Why do girls seemingly not want to play jazz outside school?

In Vicari's research 80% of respondents taught at conservatoires, 30% at universities and 10% at other locations. In these courses, women played piano, sax, guitar, flute, trombone, bass, drums, trumpet and flute. All courses had female vocalists. On the subject of the number of females auditioning, four colleges had 10-15%, one had 10-25%, one 25-40% and two 50%. The make-up of male-to-female in UK colleges varied, some figures being Royal Conservatoire of Scotland at 0%, Middlesex University 14%, Guildhall School of Music and Drama 16%, Royal Academy of Music 7%, and Royal Welsh College of Music and Drama 25%. For Trinity College of Music there were three years of figures available which showed during 2011-12, 14% were women with 4% being instrumentalists. In 2012-13, 21% were women and 9% of these were instrumentalists. For 2013-14, 20% were women and 9% of these were instrumentalists.

Figures show that quantitatively there are undeniably:

- Many more male performers comfortable in jam sessions or auditioning;
- More men coming to study jazz at degree or post graduate levels;
- More men listed as leaders or given headline billing at festivals than women.

There are barriers to women entering music and jazz music especially, and they remain set high. There may be a slight increase in the number of females studying jazz but the numbers performing and signed to labels remains low.

To add to the quantitative proof, qualitative proof was sought, and those in the know were asked for their observations.

Venues

Venues are great places to get information. Those working on the ground can see who comes to performances as well as who plays. I asked Jack Hersh of London's Jazz Cafe for his observations and he commented, "There's certainly been an issue with having women in jazz music. Traditionally there have been many factors in play. General misconceptions about who ought to be playing jazz have been the biggest barrier. The belief that jazz was a 'man's scene' prevented many females taking part, something we saw reflected in wider society for a long time".

Dr Kathianne Hingwan is General Manager of Vortex Jazz Club in Dalston, London. She told me, "As someone who has been around the Vortex for seven years, I can say from my observations that the number of women who pass through as musicians is small. The bands overwhelmingly tend to be all-male with occasionally a female member. However very few bands are female-led, or will have more than two women, let alone have female composers".

Observations from educators

Some of the best-placed people to observe what is happening at one of the main access points to jazz are those in education. The figures show that fewer students are enrolling in jazz courses, but what do those who are teaching see?

Dr Sarah Gail Brand is Professor of Improvised Music at the Guildhall School of Music and Drama. She has been on the improvised music scene for over 27 years both in the UK and abroad, and made many recordings. Therefore, she is in a good place both as an educator and musician to make some insightful observations.

On whether there was evidence to back up the concept there are far fewer female performers in UK jazz, Dr Brand replied, "I don't think it is a concept. I think it's a truth. A concept would imply it is an abstract notion that can be applied to a reality but actually it is a reality that there are far fewer female performers in jazz. There is evidence to back this up. I have seen research conducted by people like the Musicians' Union. Lots of people are doing master's research into this. In fact, I answered similar questions on this the other day for a master's research in Canterbury and it is a question I have been asked many times over the last few years and there is tons of evidence. A quick Google or Google scholar search will find the quantitative evidence, so I think it is a reality".

On whether female students are discouraged at schools or colleges, Dr Brand said, "At school, possibly. I think this has to do with young women deciding what they want to do with their life. They are encouraged to see jazz mostly as a hobby. Most people know you can't make a living out of it and girls are encouraged to be practical and stand on their own two feet these days. College is a different matter. I think if a young woman is already playing jazz by the time she is in college she's not going to get discouraged. In fact, I'm thinking of one young woman who was one of the most stunning saxophone players I have ever heard who was at Guildhall a couple of years ago. She was a fabulous musician and respected by students and tutors alike. She did incredibly well so no one discouraged her. Everyone regarded her as brilliant – and she is. I am seeing more women in the jazz courses. They tend to be vocalists and I think they get accepted on a slightly different criteria than instrumentalists. I think for vocalists, proper teaching of improvisation doesn't start until they get to college whereas with many of instrumentalists, teaching of improvisation happens before they reach higher education and those instrumentalists tend to be boys".

Sue Richardson (R) with Denys Baptiste (L) © Monika Jakubowksa

Trish Clowes © John Cronin

Chapter 4

What do Performers See?

Andrea Vicari, whose work is quoted above, is also a
performing and recording pianist and radio presenter so she
is in a good position to give her observations. On whether
there is observational evidence to back up the widely held
concept that there are far fewer female performers in UK
jazz, Vicari said, "The evidence can be seen from listings
of jazz gigs where more men are listed than women.
Reading magazines such as Jazzwise you see articles and
reviews of bands and CDs and they are mostly about men.
Women are more likely to be vocalists. As a female jazz
pianist, I tend to work in the field of jazz doing gigs and
festivals around the country and I rarely see bands with
women being advertised to play. I teach at Trinity Laban
Conservatoire where there are only two female members of
staff who teach jazz (not including vocal staff). Most of the
students are male with only a handful of female students".

Many findings can be extrapolated from studies into this
area and the facts given here are by no means conclusive.
Each study delves into a different area of gender difference
in jazz music and concentrates on different ages and
settings so a read of just a few will provide a clearer view.

There is quantitative, qualitative and anecdotal evidence
of this issue; there are unquestionably fewer women in jazz
in the UK than men. Furthermore, women appear to
disappear from jazz music and playing in jazz settings
during or around their teenage years. In schools, jazz is

popular and male and female students thrive but this parity does not follow into college or beyond. Whether the route to jazz is through college, experience or playing in a range of genres and in spite of much work being done to try to redress the disparity, female musicians are scarce.

From women

The best people to comment on the disparity in the UK jazz scene are the women working in it. Their views reflect the reality of the scene, regardless of what is spoken of academically or theoretically.

It is a fact that many of the people involved in academic studies or initiatives are adamant that much progress has been made. Talking directly to those women active in the UK jazz scene paints a slightly different picture.

The following events are a few examples, some demonstrating crass sexism is alive and well in jazz and some that there is a change in attitude. All these events took place in the last two years and highlight the different experiences of female musicians.

On one occasion a male agent considered that the best way to introduce himself to a world-class saxophone player was to stick his business card into her cleavage. This was in 2019.

A female bandleader told me about her experience with a venue where she asked about playing and was told there were no slots available. A couple of hours later, her husband – the guitar player in her band – called and spoke to the same person. He was offered a choice of slots.

A trombonist (female) had a review of one of her gigs and the reviewer ended the piece by stating, "And the most amazing thing was the trombonist was a woman!" Would they have written, "And the interesting thing was that the sax, bass, guitar and piano players were all male"?

A trumpeter answered a call-out for players in a venue in Manchester. She was told, "Oh, sorry, we have enough females on the list now". Not even an offer of an audition. To add insult to injury she was asked if she knew of any other musician (presumably male) that might want to apply to play there.

On another occasion a female singer took her band to see a venue where they had been booked to perform for a large wedding. The manager, completely serious, asked her if she could "dress a little sassy" and maybe, as she was singing, "wander around and flirt with some of the guests". Completely deadpan, the woman asked the venue manager if he would like some of the band – all male – to do the same and was greeted with, "Of course not. That is not the point". One might ask what exactly the point was.

Another female saxophone player said, "I played a gig where I was asked to look 'hot', required to wear a dress and asked to dance. High heels and an instrument do not go together. In similar situations, I questioned the organisers and was either shunted to the back of the band or just not called back".

Another scenario: a gig, a female guitar player, a sensational set. Great stuff. Socialising afterwards with the audience a man sidles up to the guitar player and says, "Wow, for a woman, you play really well".

Another time, a young singer was performing her third gig as leader of a line-up and at a much bigger venue than the band was used to. Things went well. The crowd went wild. A week later she read a review. In it, the reviewer spoke about the 'pianist bandleader' (her brother, John played piano in the band), his great playing and arrangements (they were hers), and the guitarist and drummer were mentioned (both male). The reviewer finished with, "All this was topped off by the pretty singer doing her level best and looking fabulous". Had he read the flier, he would have known the band was led by the young singer and she composed the music. Another saxophone player was accused of miming because she was so good.

The list of ignorant comments, not perhaps intended to hurt but indicative of deeply entrenched attitudes, goes on and on. These attitudes should have disappeared decades ago but far too often sexism still rears its ugly head. As a reviewer, I have got to know musicians and one of the great things is they speak freely when I'm around. After a gig at Cafe OTO in Dalston, London, I was having a social drink with some of the band members. One of them smiled, looked around and declared, "We are so lucky. We play great places, meet good people and the women are fantastic when they are all dolled up in their finery".

At the same time, there have been occasions when women have experienced no discrimination. It must be remembered that historically and today there have been and are men who are very aware of the women whom they play with. There are men and women who work together on an equal footing and there are men and women who actively encourage women to play jazz and offer them opportunities to do so (more on this later).

Guitarist, pianist, composer, vocalist and bandleader Faye Patton said her young male band members treat her

with great respect. Female bandleaders like Kim Cypher
find they are given respect by band members and audiences
alike so whilst there are examples of ignorance and
disrespect for females, this is largely being replaced by
behaviours which are more acceptable today. The fact that
nowadays when sexism happens, it gets called out and
commented on shows it is becoming rarer.

It is still true though that many women drop out of the
profession because they find an intrinsic lack of
opportunities for females. There is a subconscious
discrimination which is very difficult to tackle. Anyone
attending concerts might see examples. At a gig in 2017 I
observed as a band invited friends to come up and play in
the final set. In the audience were about 16 men and
women with their instruments who had been told this
would happen. Eight of the 10 men present were asked to
join the band on stage, but just one of the six women was
invited up. So many women feel they are not given the
same chances their male counterparts are – even by jazz
bands themselves.

It is interesting hearing from a woman just breaking into
jazz in the UK. Kat Lee Ryan of the Fabulous Red Diesel
says, "I am trying to break into the scene so I have quite a
bottom-up view. I think there is a bias towards females
being solo vocalists and men doing the more band-based
music. I don't see many female-fronted and led jazz bands,
which is what I do myself".

On possible reasons why, Ryan says, "Maybe it is
because women are taken less seriously as musicians. You
have to fight your corner most of the time to be seen as a
musician rather than a female. I don't see men having that

problem; their ability and talent is taken for granted by other men".

For Kat, school was encouraging. It was afterwards that she found a lack of support. She comments, "In both school and college I was totally encouraged, but once I left, I found that I was treated firstly like eye candy with no musical knowledge (which is not the case) or taken less seriously by some bookers".

Pianist, educator and bandleader Claire Cope sums up the choice of instrument at an early age, the difficulties of being a female musician, the importance of looking at the bigger picture and the movement away from women being in the minority and gaining more visibility when she says, "The question of whether I have faced obstacles as a female jazz musician is a challenging one. On the one hand, some of my biggest encouragers and supporters have been men and of course I appreciate greatly the wonderful male musicians I have played with in the past, and play with presently. I think the issue really goes to the roots of how the world gender-defines music, genres and instruments from an early age. It is undeniable that there has been historically a pervading masculine energy within the jazz scene; one that could be perceived as intimidating to women. I think it is important to note that there are so many other aspects to being a musician that present challenges.

"The social aspect of playing in bands, for instance, where women are often in the minority, may not always be enjoyable and I have, on occasion, encountered a certain sense of isolation that comes with that. However, I think we are moving away from this now as there are a multitude of female musicians and composers who are working at the highest level. The key to this is visibility; I truly believe that women thrive when they see other women thriving".

From men

A male jazz player who asked to remain anonymous shared his opinion: "It's really depressing how fixated on gender people are and how it affects decisions that they make. I have been sacked from two jobs for being male, one about twenty years ago, from a children's orchestra. They were very open about it and far from apologetic. They offered me the job as a brass tutor and then withdrew the offer when they realised they had a quota of male/female to make or they wouldn't qualify for some grant or other. It really upset me at the time and I vowed never to make a professional decision, ever, based on gender".

He went on to say, "Recently, a band that I have given loyal service to for 10 years decided that they wanted to diversify. They were worried about criticism for only having one to two females on stage, so I was let go so that they could find another female player".

Men also take note of what happens to females in their bands. One male musician recalled the story of one of his band members, a brilliant sax player. "She hates to talk about it", he divulged, "but in previous years she has had to wear a short skirt and play horrible jazz licks to a DJ in corporate gigs. I think that the problem she had with it was being booked for her looks rather than her talent on the sax".

More recently, men are beginning to feel that, with the onus being put on equality, there is potentially discrimination against them. They say it is because venues need to appear 'politically correct' (and the figures for some festivals tell us how well *that* one is going). One man told me he was sure he had lost out to women because there are fewer of them and a demand that more are seen, so they find it easier to get a place in a festival line-up. I asked him if he had any proof. He told me, "No, but you just kind of know when you are discriminated against, don't you?"

Another musician said he had been asked to leave his tutoring position in a school because they wanted to encourage more female brass players. He said it was a double blow because he actively encouraged girls who wanted to play brass instruments, but was told they had found a female tutor who could teach and provide a role model for the girls.

On another occasion, a man remembered a time when he lost his place in a band he had played with for a long time because they wanted to use a female musician in order to bring more diversity to the band. "They told me, to my face", he said, "they wanted a woman".

What about LGBTQ+ musicians?

It is important to be aware that being 'male' or 'female' is not always binary. You can be 'male' or 'female' yet not fall within society's expectations of what that might mean. You may not identify as male or female and you may not have characteristics or behaviour expected of your born gender. So how do you fit in? Where are you in all this?

Graham J is a male alto with a string of successes. He has played Broadway and major venues in the UK and across the globe. He also happens to be a gay man.

On whether his sexual identity was something he felt was important in his performance, Graham said, "This is an interesting area. It's not as straightforward an answer as 'yes' or 'no'. I would say it certainly helps inform my choice of repertoire and my song writing. My sexual orientation, being a part of my psyche, helps inform my emotional and spiritual world which obviously colours the choices I make as an artist and how I choose to interpret a lyric or melody. As a singer, my responsibility is to convey as much meaning as possible; to sing with truth. That truth must be mine. That doesn't mean that I couldn't sing a song about or play the part of someone whose sexuality differs from mine. Singing is acting. You have to internalise things and relate them to your own experiences. However, during an actual performance, it doesn't matter. My job is to give to my audience. They've paid for me to take them out of their own heads for a few hours".

On whether it matters if the audience knows he is gay. Graham said, "I'm an openly gay man so my audience generally knows this. I don't think it's important for them as such. It informs my artistic choices but the contract we performers have with an audience is to entertain them; to give them pleasure, pain and succour; to allow them a respite from their own thoughts or to help them connect with others. I know when I go to a concert and listen to another artist perform I'm not thinking about their sexuality or gender for that matter. I'm there for my own selfish reasons. I want to listen to them perform; to hear them sing to my soul. I want to listen and feel things whether it's joyful or sad. Once music is given over to the audience it's down to them to internalise it. At that moment, all that really concerns a listener is what's in their own head. They don't need or really want to know what's going on in mine".

Graham has experienced discrimination but not by audiences. He explains, "I haven't had discrimination from venues or festivals. The only time I've experienced discrimination was when a reviewer for a well-known magazine wrote a disgusting personal attack on my sexuality. As I said at the time, I'm not bothered if he liked or disliked my music. It didn't give him the right to write homophobic slurs saying that I was 'limp-wristed' etc. Most people aren't bothered anymore. People just want good music".

The review Graham spoke of was indeed an awful one for a British jazz journal to publish. It spoke of the reviewer's conclusion that, after listening to the first part of a song, Graham had his metatarsal removed at birth. The magazine removed the offensive lines after complaints but there was no apology or understanding shown and the reviewer's apology was more on the lines of "I am sorry if you took it that way but it was my opinion".

Graham has his own opinions on why people feel the need to discriminate. He says, "I genuinely believe it's learned behaviour mixed with fear of change. We're not born hating. To quote Morgan Freeman, 'It's not a phobia. You're not scared. You're an a**hole'. I think people who are afraid to embrace change are afraid of losing control. In our industry there are a lot of people who have had things their own way for far too long. They want jazz to stay in a time warp where it doesn't evolve past their personal taste. They have very clear ideas about how things should be.

When they aren't, the knives come out and nasty things are said and done. Mostly, though, I find our music to be very supportive. The very nature of what we do allows us to push boundaries and evolve. People are constantly exploring their own truths and are quite happy for other artists to do the same".

On whether the growing awareness of gender inequality in jazz was creating a bias towards female performers, Graham said, "One of my singing teachers, Dr Veronica Dunne, used to tell me there are nine million sopranos in the world. Maybe I'm being naive but I've always believed there are more female singers than male. I don't think that there has been a sudden rush to programme more female and LGBTQ artists over cisgender heterosexual male artists. In my experience there just happen to be more female artists to choose from [for singers]. At the end of the day I believe bookers and clubs want the best acts. They want packed houses and to make money. I think and hope that they are more concerned with quality and longevity than gender politics and quotas. As a singer who has worked in various genres, I've been lucky enough to be surrounded by some incredible female colleagues. Looking back on my career, the industry, for me, has always been dominated by a strong female presence. Teachers, colleagues, and band mates. I am blest amongst women as it were".

Faye Patton is not only a bandleader, she is a gifted musician who composes music for her quartet as well as her solo sets. We had a long discussion after one of her performances and several people joined us. "For the majority of people", said Patton, "gender is no longer just binary. Sometimes, you have to choose how you approach a role – as a man or a woman? It depends how you feel you are being treated. As an LGBT person I experience the world from male and female viewpoints. Maybe women could think of a situation and wonder what they would do if they were a man. Would they fight more, not care if they slipped up, not apologise for errors, confidently close a deal?

"It can pay to use 'female' qualities – be nice, sweet, gentle. That works in some situations but in others, it pays to use the 'male' qualities, so fight for your right, be stronger maybe. Whatever, the connection to the music and audience is important. Let them in and trust in the music".

Patton is aware of organisations and individuals working to improve the situation for women in UK jazz. She mentioned Tomorrow's Warriors, Women in Jazz and Georgia Mancio who campaigns for equality and holding the press accountable. One thing Patton felt was important was there should be more female-owned clubs like The Green Note in Camden, London.

On the LGBTQ community within jazz, she says there is growing support. Indeed, when I last met up with her, she was playing to an audience of LGBTQ community jazz meet-up members and the atmosphere was like a party. I found, due to some elaborate dresses, fancy feathers and flounced skirts, it was difficult to always know whether you were chatting with a man or woman. And it became irrelevant because after a while, you just concentrated on the person. The warmth and support for Patton was tangible. We got on to the subject of women going alone to gigs and feeling in the minority. One of the male guests batted his false eyelashes, smoothed his dress, fixed me with a stare, arching his perfectly formed eyebrows and said, "YOU feel odd?" I took his point.

There are LGBTQ festivals and opportunities to perform, for example at Pride (an annual celebration of equality and diversity). There is also Queer and Unsigned which describes itself as "a universal platform for all queer artists to showcase their work, network and be absolutely fabulous! Also a place for anyone who loves good art, music, performance and all things artistic to discover the best up and coming artists and events from the LGBTQ+ community". Patton relishes the advent of organisations like this but adds there is no sustained infrastructure and initiatives come and go without any real funding, plans for longevity or ability to offer artists anything beyond the event itself.

She also commented on the gender disparity on a recent Ronnie Scott's programme. "Here is my serious concern. The latest season seems to have programmed very, very few women. I mean really hardly any. It's embarrassing. Doesn't Ronnie's know about the great UK female performers in the UK, right here? Are they not engaged with what is going on under their noses? There are so many fantastic female musicians, singers, instrumentalists and bandleaders out there right now who audiences want to see. There are many who should be regular faces at London's most famous jazz clubs. I'd like to see Ayanna Witter-Johnson, Nikki Yeoh, Juliet Kelly, Julie Dexter, Janette Mason or any of the Blow the Fuse crew".

Patton's ideas for improving the situation are that "women have to demand more and not be so grateful for small concessions. We need support and mentoring networks, databases and information hubs. Informal and formal networking and our own equivalent of the old-boy networks".

Patton is right. The list of UK female musicians is extensive and we should be seeing more at major venues. For example, guitarists Nora Bite, Rosie Frater-Taylor, Shirley Tetteh, Sherika Sherard, Deirdre Cartwright, bass players Yolanda Charles (Mama Yo) and Alison Rayner. Pianists Nikki Iles, Kate Williams and Janette Mason, keyboard player Jessica Lauren, drummers Sophie Alloway and Abbie Finn, harp player Alina Bzhezhinska, sax player YolanDa Brown, 'cello player Shirley Smart, trombonists Sarah Gail Brand and Annie Whitehead, trumpeter Yazz Ahmed and vocalists Zeeteah Massiah, Sarah Jane Morris, Niki King, Tamar Osborn, Julie Dexter and Zara McFarlane. For any club to be unaware of these and many more female UK jazz musicians shows a detachment from what is happening right where they are based and if you look at other scenes like Scotland, Ireland, Northern England and the West Country, there are female musicians who are amazing – and local.

Surely it is a simple thing. If a musician is a poor or great performer, their sexual orientation or gender identity is probably one of the least influences on the mastery of their instrument. There are, however, many supremely talented female jazz musicians in the UK and not enough of them are seen performing regularly.

Is there female bias?

With festivals and other events being encouraged to increase the visibility of female performers, is there a chance that there might be discrimination against men in favour of women? If 50:50 gender parity is to be achieved soon, the number of women on stage is going to have to increase massively. The only way to do this would be to earnestly recruit women. Is there then a danger of bias in favour of women?

Dr Hingwan of Vortex Jazz Club says, "I don't think there is an emerging bias towards female players. You could presumably make the same case for musicians of colour. It's more a case of 'well let's see what you can do if given the chance'. There are women performers who hate the gender prefix *female* pianist, *female* saxophonist because before a single note has been performed the music has already been gendered and labelled 'weak and insipid'. I agree the prefix is a nuisance. I find that because the number of women in jazz forms a small pool from which to draw on, one consequence is the tendency to see the same female players. We need to add more to the pool".

I asked Andrea Vicari whether she was aware of a bias towards female musicians because of the need to change. She replied, "This is a hard one and the answer could be yes. The jazz industry relies on public money even if in small quantities and therefore organisations in receipt of public funds need to show a programme that reflects the population in the UK. This means programmes have to have a certain [number] of bands that are either led by women or feature women in order to demonstrate no discrimination. This is welcomed by women as it encourages female musicians to lead bands and feel part of the jazz community. However, there is also a sense that given there are so few female jazz musicians they have a much easier time promoting their groups and getting gigs compared to their male counterparts. With this comes a feeling that they aren't as good because they are only getting the gig because they are women. This argument has probably been used against ethnic minorities too. Often the attitude of minorities is the opposite in that they feel they have to be twice as good to prove themselves in a field where they are in few numbers".

Vocalist, saxophone player, composer and bandleader Kim Cypher, on the other hand, has seen little evidence of bias. She comments, "I can only speak from my personal experience and have no evidence to suggest there has been bias towards me as a female performer. I would like to think that artists are booked purely on the merit of their music and performance. This is certainly how it should be. Perhaps this growing awareness has brought people's attention to the fact that all artists should be treated with equal respect but I would hope the music and performance is always the deciding factor".

However, more generally, there is in reality little chance of discriminating either way because the pool of female jazz musicians is tiny. Dr Brand, who as well as being an educator is also a bandleader, told me, "I am aware myself of not having many women in my ensembles. In fact in both the ensembles I have been running recently, there are no women apart from me. People say to me 'there are no women in your band' and I say 'there's me and I'm the bandleader.' This is largely down to the fact I choose musicians who can reflect the kind of music I want performed and because women haven't been given those opportunities; those women haven't existed so far in my career. Those women are probably there but I haven't heard of them because they haven't been pushed forward. I don't know of anyone in the UK or anywhere at the moment who can play like, for example, Mark Sanders [drummer]. If there was a woman who can play exactly like him I would want to work with her. It's the drumming I want; the understanding of improvisation and jazz intertwined. Once I actually meet women who are able to play that way I will be rushing to form a band with them. There are women I do like working with. I have worked with them and been in ensembles with them and I think they are brilliant. People like Rachel Musson and Charlotte Keeffe are great musicians but at the moment they are not playing the sounds for me and the ensembles. Rachel plays tenor saxophone and I tend not to use saxophones. So it is to do with the pool of musicians available that I want to work with. The kind of sounds I like are often played by men simply because more men are playing that way and women haven't been encouraged to. In improvised music as opposed to just jazz, there are even fewer women; though there are some coming through, there aren't as many as there ought to be so it is still a very limited pool sadly".

Echoing Dr Brand's experience, Joy Ellis told me she does discriminate in favour of women at times, explaining, "The musicians in my band are male but when I need a replacement musician I actively discriminate in favour of women – which is not wrong because I am not permanently changing the band members, but so far it has been hard to find a guitar player who plays the music I like. I can find bass players; there is a larger pool of good female bassists but not so many guitarists".

Dr Brand surmises her thoughts when she says, "The question is whether male jazz musicians are being discriminated against. My joke might be to ask, 'oh, male jazz musicians; will anyone ever give them a break?' Jazz has been biased towards male musicians since it started over 100 years ago. I am fine about jazz being biased towards female performers for a change. If there is a notion that men are feeling oppressed by acts of equality, then it means they regard equality as oppression because they have enjoyed privilege for so long. It makes me quite annoyed that the question even exists in the first place. What would tip the scales would be if you only ever saw women performing. For as long as men continue to outnumber women in bands, festivals, programmes for jazz clubs and in recordings and every possible sphere of jazz and improvised music-making, there needs to be women-focused funding and women-focused programmes. There needs to be positive, active engagement of women in jazz and improvised women in order to balance the scale and I frankly don't give a damn if men feel victimised or not – it's like, 'welcome to the bloody party'. That's all I can say".

Faye Patton © Benjamin John

Graham J © Jonathan Phang

Vick Bain © Andrew Laming

Joy Ellis © Pedro Valasco

Andrea Vicari courtesy of the artist

Chapter 5

Why Women Aren't Visible in UK Jazz

There is no difference in the ability of women and men to improvise and physically, no reason why anyone cannot play any instrument they want to. So there must be other reasons for the current lack of women in UK jazz.

Women make up roughly 50% of the population. No music genre is going to remain popular if it only appeals to and welcomes half the population. Women contribute more now to financing the jazz industry by supporting venues or buying merchandise, downloads and physical recordings. They may support their partner if they are a musician by having a steady career. The jazz industry needs to understand the increasing strength of the female pound. Women have their own money to spend how they wish – and hopefully, they will be encouraged to spend some of it on jazz but jazz first has to become more attractive to them.

Women bring qualities to jazz; a different viewpoint, different ways of hearing, seeing and understanding the music which benefit and enrich jazz in a way which expands its appeal. Women represent an increasingly powerful element of society and jazz music has historically reflected societal changes and reaction. It is only right that more women should be in jazz. So, where are they?

Dr Sarah Gail Brand comments, "I think there's the question of 'do we know there are fewer female performers in UK jazz or do we just think there are because the men are more famous and well-known and it is normalised that men play jazz?' It is accepted that men are the pioneers and the enablers of pioneers over the last few years. I think a lot of it has to do with the historiography of jazz; the way jazz has been written about. In the 1940s, 50s and 60s there were women working. There was Valaida Snow the trumpet player, there was Melba Liston, who was an incredible trombonist and arranger and she was also in the Jazz Messengers with Archie Shepp so there are many important women. There haven't been as many as men but again this is because of the social mores of the times. There are many more women that have and do play jazz across the world. It is just that there is an unconscious social decision to not talk about them".

Historically in the UK, the managers and owners of clubs and other venues have been largely male and have tended to appoint male programmers. Dr Hingwan says, "The Vortex has always had a male programmer until recently. However, now with three people involved in the programming, two are male, one is female. Also there are not many female musicians. I saw somewhere only 6% of students studying jazz in the conservatoires were women. Imagine what the percentage for black and female is. You could say there was an inherent male bias. However, if you consider the type of music the club is known for [free jazz and improvised music] they tend to be genres that are male-dominated anyway. In more straight-ahead jazz if there is a woman in the band they are mostly likely to be the vocalist.[14] The musicians tend to represent an older generation".

---

[14] Female singers fronting a band but given little importance used to be dubbed "canaries" because of their ornamental value. Many straight-ahead jazz bands have

On whether female musicians are faring any better, Dr Hingwan continues, "Female representation improves slightly but women still remain overwhelmingly under-represented. No seismic changes here. Why? Is there a female style of playing and male style of playing that influence audience preferences? I've never heard anyone actually voice this but I suspect that some people believe it, in line with general discourses about women's inferiority and feeble female playing".

This is powerful stuff but, considering the evidence is based on Dr Hingwan's experience of over seven years at Vortex, it makes interesting reading. She goes on to explain what people believe about jazz and the general stereotyping of players by saying, "Jazz is the preserve of the male player who has the muscularity to pull it off. Then, can we say women's jazz is not as good as male jazz? No, rubbish! If you listen to a piece of the music with your eyes closed can you guess the gender of the musicians? Probably not. This is more likely to be based on stereotypical views that some instruments are seen to be more suited to men than women. At my time at the club I have only seen one female drummer". This is a shame when you consider that female drummers have proved themselves some of the world's best – Viola Smith, Cindy Blackman and Terri Lyne Carrington are just a few female drummers whose talent traverses the decades.

Many women talk about feeling they have to go to extra lengths to prove themselves in jazz. If a woman is an

---

females as backing vocalists but they are given little to do in the way of harmonies or technical improvisation.

excellent musician, playing different genres, jazz might hold little appeal if her talent is constantly brought into question when she tries out in jazz. This might lead to fewer talented female musicians playing jazz. After all, if even if they work hard, they may never feel fully accepted so some may ask themselves, 'why bother? '

Underlying reasons for male dominance in jazz – male privilege

In 1989 in her book "Stormy Weather"[15] Linda Dahl writes, "Still, the male jazz musician accepts and takes for granted that at every step he'll be dealing with other men – from club owners to booking agents to bandleaders, fellow players, reviewers and writers in the press: a male-dominated profession. The language that describes jazz, and jazz musicians, reflects this reality….The actor in this world of music is with good reason commonly called the 'jazzman'". This perhaps sums up past thinking well.

There is a historical view that being feminine is incompatible with being a jazz musician. The roots of gender bias in jazz go back to well before it became a recognised genre. Until the early twentieth century and in many ways later, women were viewed as homemakers, supporters and mothers whose place was at home. The public did not welcome women as solo artists, with the exception of a few ballet stars and opera singers. Some women were accepted as pianists, singers and violinists but more 'masculine' instruments such as brass, woodwind or

[15] Dahl, Linda. "Stormy Weather: The Music and Lives of a Century of Jazz Women". Publisher: Limelight Editions (Pantheon Books), ISBN 978-0-3945-3555-5 (1984).

heaven forbid, drums, were discouraged. Women could not, it was believed, be expected to wield a large instrument like a double bass or understand the technical intricacies of harmonics. These stereotypical view of women might partially explain why, historically, women seem to have been written out of the media records. A singer is very visible on stage but their status has been seen as lower than those who play instruments.

Jazz solos, especially in the bebop era, were fast, frenetic and forceful, with multiple key changes and an aggressive style which favoured male musicians.

It could also be that jazz emerged from an almost entirely male subculture at a time when women had few privileges and reputation was everything, so they were less likely to visit clubs and nighttime hangs like bottle clubs and speakeasies where the music was played. Jazz was linked to hard drugs and alcohol, making it an unattractive prospect for women. Later, jazz became more intellectual, with white male musicians such as Dave Brubeck, Paul Desmond and Gil Evans gaining endorsements and fame. Women were not encouraged into this arena either.

When jazz became popular, the clubs' cutting contests were almost exclusively male events held late at night when women would not have access to the spaces. The whole set-up favoured male dominance and success.

Books written about jazz tend to concentrate not on the vibrant, colourful history but rather portray jazz as played by men with women mentioned as insignificant 'others', perhaps the piano player or singer. Rather than telling readers about the changing, diverse scene of today, books are more likely to concentrate on the history, trying to form some rigid, steady progression of the music. Readers learn that women, whilst present, were marginalised, on the sidelines. So their education starts.

In the UK during the 1950s and 1960s, jazz was divided. There were traditionalists favouring New Orleans-style jazz bands led by players including Humphrey Lyttelton and Chris Barber. There was also modern jazz with an emphasis on bebop individualistic style, whose supporters included Ronnie Scott and John Dankworth and players preferring freer styles influenced by US and European jazz. All these subgenres were male-dominated. In the freer playing bands, the music was aggressive, strong and antagonistic. Some jazz musicians became involved in marches and protests, at the time not places for women. Male musicians went to America from the UK and brought back different playing styles they heard in clubs like the Five Spot. There were fall-outs with the American Federation of Musicians which involved entrepreneurial solutions by influential people such as Ronnie Scott and Peter King. The point is there were male musicians taking risks, jumping ship in America (like Ken Colyer) so they could sit in clubs and find new jazz sounds, where incidentally men were also running the clubs.

During the 1960s jazz became associated with politics, especially in Europe. Players including Peter Brötzmann, Sven-Åke Johansson and Han Bennink led an energetic, physical form of playing which was explorative and masculine. Discussing the period with Brötzmann led to an understanding of why the playing was so explosive – it was a reaction against the war and what the previous generations had done, and to the race riots in America; but it was very much the young male musician on the road who led this movement. Brötzmann explained that in Europe in those days a musician could travel for weeks and get a gig nearly every night. More recently, free jazz players have welcomed female players and the current generation is more accepting of all humanity into the expressive music. Free players like Mats Gustafsson, Terry Day and Evan Parker collaborate with male and female musicians (and writers).

Several women have spoken of a lingering, almost subconscious attitude from male musicians which shows itself in the language they use. One elderly jazz musician commented, "There are far fewer women around, it is true, but the really good ones force their way to the front". Is he saying men don't force their way? Another woman told me of a manager who said to her, "The problem is people still expect a woman to add a touch of gentleness, glamour and be good-looking. Sorry, but there it is. A guy can be bearded, sweaty, dishevelled and the size of a walrus and he will be applauded if he is good. If a woman came on stage looking the same (minus the beard of course) the audience would be so shocked her playing style wouldn't get a mention. It is just how things are, get over it".

The sociology behind the lack of women in UK jazz

On whether she thought there were sociological reasons behind the lack of females in jazz, Andrea Vicari comments, "There are many reasons including cultural and family expectations. Traditionally girls were pushed into careers that were 'safe' and where there were already women succeeding. Jazz has mostly male role models and so wouldn't be seen as a career for a woman in some households. Improvisation, if not experienced at a young age or in an encouraging environment, can be difficult for girls if they are not confident. There are also social pressures and expectations which often discourage girls to take risks in their teenage years which is what often happens when you 'take a solo'. Working late hours for little money doesn't always fit in with the female lifestyle, especially when women decide to have families. Many professional women manage both, but in my personal experience there are many women who play jazz who don't have children and maybe they are more successful in their careers because they didn't procreate".

On finding work, Vicari says, "Working in the jazz world is difficult and it is hard for anyone, male or female, to survive. Funding is not easy to get and there are very few easy ways to become established. There are no funded jazz orchestras or a funded jazz centre. People tend to work with their friends and there are no auditions for work.

"Men tend to book men and it's hard for women to make a stand against this because in the end the reason (they are told) will be because men are better at playing jazz. It has been a self-perpetuating cycle which hadn't been broken until jazz education became formalised. As a female jazz pianist my entire career has been playing mostly in either all-female bands, bands led by females (often vocalists) and bands led by Afro-Caribbean musicians. One exception is a band that is led by a Croatian male guitarist who booked me and has repeatedly booked me as he (and his wife) found me on the internet when looking for

interesting musicians to bring to Croatia on an arts
exchange programme".

Vicari adds a more positive note by saying,
"My experiences are not the same as the younger
generations who have had access to a formal jazz
education. With jazz degrees in the UK having been around
for 30 years, female jazz musicians are working more
closely with male musicians and there seems to be a more
accepting attitude towards working together. A clear access
to a profession makes it possible for minorities to succeed.
Sadly, even though women are 50% of the population when
it comes to playing jazz, they are a minority. In the old
days, the way into jazz was through jam sessions and who
knew who, which didn't provide an easy route for many
women".

Sociologically, things seem to have changed over the
past decade – and in a very positive way. A woman who
studied jazz 15 years ago shared her experience. "Loads of
the male professors flirted with us girls. One or two had
flings with students. They never gave them importance the
way they did the male students and once or twice I voiced
an opinion, only to be smirked at. When a guy raised the
same issue, it was discussed. Also, what they don't teach
you is how to get a job afterwards. Or how to manage the
money side of things. Or how to deal with being the only
woman on the gig, a tour, etc. It can get very lonely to be
frank and it would have been great to hear from female
musicians who had been there, done that. Sadly, the only
female teacher I ever saw was a German 'cello tutor who I
heard playing jazz in one of the practice rooms. I asked if I

could play with her and she laughed and said she only taught classical".

There are, however, people who support female students who demonstrate an interest in jazz. Recently a female student on a classical degree course at Leeds Conservatoire told me that when she showed a liking for jazz music her tutor encouraged her, taking the attitude that so long as you are progressing and developing your music, the genre is irrelevant. He introduced her to students on the jazz study course and they began playing together in ensembles. The student has now graduated and regularly plays jazz gigs in London. Whilst she still plays classical music, jazz is now an option for her thanks to her forward-thinking tutor.

Could it be there are deeper sociological reasons for women not being visible in UK jazz? There is a theory called the 'circle of oppression' where a group who feels in the minority will have a fear of being different. The majority in the group assigns the minority group traits such as being subordinate or not being as talented or clever. The minority internalise and subconsciously take on the attributes expected of them by the majority whilst also trying to take on some attributes of the majority. If a new member of the minority group joins them, they criticise them for being different. The circle therefore continues.

Dr Brand puts the blame squarely on sociological reasons. She says, "There are purely sociological reasons behind the lack of women in UK jazz. There are no biological reasons, that's for sure. There are no deficits in women's ability to play jazz and there isn't a superior ability in men naturally, so it is utterly sociological and societal. I think the reason behind there not being as many women performing jazz or known to be performing jazz in this country is misogyny. I have said this so many times and people think it is a bit harsh but I do believe that hatred of women is one of the reasons women weren't engaged by men to play in the first place and why women aren't taken seriously as artists of complex music.

"Many men believe women are not capable of mastering the complexity of jazz. By complexity, I mean the underlying harmonic properties of jazz: form, time, groove, specificity of instruments, ability, that kind of thing. There will be examples of women being openly discouraged, as in, 'you can't play this, you're a girl' or 'we don't let women play jazz' maybe 20 or 30 years ago but I think nowadays women are not openly discouraged, but there is nothing in society which actually encourages them. I mean, there are initiatives and research questions like this but as long as we are still having to ask the question 'why are there fewer female performers in UK jazz?' it means there are fewer female performers in UK jazz.

"I think what would improve things is if jazz itself was more supported in society and then women would regard it as a serious profession but younger women have been encouraged over the last 30 years to be more independent and not need men to financially support them or give them a sense of self. The flip side of that is many male musicians have famously married women in jobs so they can earn a stable income whilst men go off and pursue the uncertain employment world of jazz. Can you imagine a situation where a man would be prepared to do that for a woman? Some men do that for women but society is not ready for this to be considered as the norm – again down to the fact that women are not liked very much. There is also the added sociological complexity of women not wanting women to play jazz – by women I mean girlfriends and wives of men who play jazz – unless there is a deep bond of trust between the women jazz musicians and a relationship between her and the partner of the male musician. It tends to be that female partners of male jazz musicians do not like the men inviting women on tour if the wives and girlfriends themselves aren't being invited. I have been in that situation a few times".

Thinking about the fall-off in the number of female musicians compared to boys in the teenage years, the explanation may lie in our development and social awareness. Jazz is a music which requires expression and emotional, hormone-charged boys seem much better at using noise to do this than girls. Dr Brand notes also the awkwardness which happens between girls and boys in teenage years: "When I have taught the Essex Youth Jazz Orchestra on a few occasions, I noticed that in the breaks the boys carry on jamming together whilst the girls stand there looking a bit left out. Boys are not going to go up to girls and say, 'Would you like to play with us?' and teenage girls are unlikely to go and offer themselves to be part of their jamming ensembles because boys and girls at that age are still trying to get to know who they are and work out what girls and boys mean to each other. This means they are unlikely to play together unless one of them is particularly up for it and confident enough to push themselves forward".

This is also seen with other jazz settings. A recent post-gig jam upstairs at Ronnie Scott's saw mostly male musicians freely play with each other whilst the women sat waiting to be asked. There were three women and around 20 men. Maybe one answer would be to leave gender identity at the door on occasions like this and simply be a musician, not caring about the gender of any of the musicians (including yourself) but this is hard when there are 90% males and 10% females present.

Are we still affected by social conditioning? Two or three generations ago when women were less assertive, to be confident was often labelled as 'aggressive' or 'bossy'. Women were, and in many ways still are, expected to nurture and teach, not to become leaders.

Gender is only part of a musician's identity. How we view anyone will be distorted if we reduce them to any parts of their identity, be it their gender, sexual orientation, ethnicity or anything else. However, to ignore these facets, be it in jazz history or today's jazz scene, is proof of neglect as well.

Is there a psychological element at play? Does the very lack of women being visible in the first place feed the misconception that jazz is 'male' even amongst women?

In activities where women perceive the activity to be more suited to men, their anxiety and lack of confidence increases. This is borne out by the number of women surveyed by Ellis and Osmianski who said they felt uncomfortable in jam sessions. However, if women have support from other musicians, parents and teachers, they become more confident. The atmosphere in a male-dominated environment in which women do not feel supported and have to prove their worthiness is not conducive to excellent and confident participation.

There are so many historical and social barriers to women's participation in jazz that contribute to their underrepresentation in most jazz settings. We need to recognise these issues are present and are limitations which male musicians do not have to deal with on the same level, therefore they may not be able to understand them. Until we acknowledge the barriers and decide to do something, gender parity in jazz will remain a long way off.

Jazz came to the UK already loaded with a history of male dominance. Women, though, love the music too and just like other previously male-dominated careers, women have every right to be there, and to be successful.

Parental perceptions

The perception of gender is instilled in us from a young age and studies such as those by Anne M. Koenig[16] have shown that gender description pretty much follows stereotypical formats regardless of age or gender. We have perceptions of what is 'appropriate' for our gender and our parents (deliberately or unwittingly) reinforce this perception in us as children.

On the topic of instruments, many female instrumentalists say they are often presumed to be a singer or gain a lot of attention being, for example, a trumpet player or double bass player. Some feel they have to prove their ability on an instrument because many people assume they might not be good. Often you still hear the phrase

---

[16] Koenig, Anne M. "Comparing Prescriptive and Descriptive Gender Stereotypes About Children, Adults, and the Elderly", Frontiers in Psychology, 2018
https://www.frontiersin.org/articles/10.3389/fpsyg.2018.01086/full

"you play well, for a woman". Jazz still carries with it connotations (incorrect, of course) of being for unschooled musicians, implying you do not need to be skilled to play jazz; it is associated, still, with drink and drugs and is played in pubs and clubs; not places parents want to encourage their girls to play in.

Parental perceptions can be very influential on children when making choices. They are more likely to allow boys to study jazz than girls. There is still sexism within families, with parents having the stereotypical view of jazz musicians as poor, drug addicts and/or alcoholics who lead lives that are incompatible with family life. With no personal experience of the modern jazz scene to go on, many adults perpetuate old-fashioned misconceptions about jazz music and players. By doing this, they inadvertently limit choices for their children. The reality is that being a jazz musician is rarely lucrative but you can earn a living by being a little creative in your work. Drugs and alcohol may have been prominent in the past but today's jazz musicians are just as likely to be teetotaling, drug-free and very aware of health issues.

The life of a musician can be very fulfilling and the benefits of doing something you love can be more important than merely working to earn money. Finally, having a family has become less a woman's job and many men now share childcare if not taking on the entire child-rearing job, so this shouldn't be a reason for not pursuing a career in jazz music, although ignoring cultural issues can be very difficult for some women.

Choice of instrument

By the time a female musician decides she is going to specialise in jazz, she needs to be able to play a suitable instrument. Of course, many people take up an instrument later in life but for the majority, their first instrument is chosen whilst they are at school. Dr Hingwan believes musical instrument choice is really important. "I think there is a perception that certain instruments 'suit women' and others 'suit men'", she says. "For young girls this could have something to do with conventional ideas about femininity".

It is not only the choice of instruments but also the perception that some instruments suit jazz whilst others do not, and that the majority of those suited to jazz are from instruments given the 'male' connotation. In a 2004 study by Kathleen McKeage[17] senior lecturer in the Department of Music at the University of Wyoming, titled "Gender and Participation in High School Instrumental Jazz Ensembles", it was found that in high school 52% of women and 80% of men surveyed reported playing jazz but by the time they got to college the figures were 14% of women and 50% of men. Again, there is that larger drop-off by women in their late teens. The reasons women gave for quitting jazz included limited choices for their primary instrument, institutional obstacles that narrowed participation options, feeling more comfortable in traditional ensembles, and an inability to connect jazz participation to career progression.

I believe musical preferences are influenced at a very young age and have much to do with teachers, syllabus

---

[17] McKeage, K. M. "Gender and Participation in High School and College Instrumental Jazz Ensembles", Journal of Research in Music Education, Issue 52 (2004): 343–356.

requirements and the kind of music people choose to expose children to. Family and other circumstances can have a big effect on music choices. As an example, I shall relate my own experience. As a child, my elder sister was a prodigiously talented pianist, appearing in local papers, winning festival classes, gaining LGSM (Licentiate of the Guildhall School of Music and Drama, a prestigious performance award) at a ridiculously young age and so on. I grew up with classical music playing a lot at home. I found piano difficult and decided to play clarinet and oboe, which was encouraged. Because I was exposed to classical music, I thought these instruments were only for playing that kind of music. My parents' musical tastes ran to classical, light opera and occasional lighter popular music, but I only ever heard jazz played in the background or on film soundtracks. I believed jazz and swing were played by huge bands or smaller groups who closed out TV shows like Acker Bilk and his band or Kenny Ball and his Jazzmen. At school, I had a talented 'cellist named Martin Felton and the redoubtable musical all-rounder Elizabeth Dutton as music teachers. I was encouraged to play oboe in the school orchestra and clarinet in a youth orchestra, to sing in the school choir, join an opera group and enter music festival folk singing competitions. Even when I balked at the idea of solo work on the oboe, I was given little choice and played "Scena" from Swan Lake and other classical works – badly and without enthusiasm.

By the time I got to university, I was encouraged to join another operatic group, performing works like Gluck's "Orfeo ed Euridice" and enter more folk competitions (which I won and was presented a cup by the since-

disgraced Mr. Rolf Harris). I was offered parts in the
Gilbert and Sullivan Society and even applied for a
scholarship which would mean I earned a little extra money
singing in the chapel choir (which I failed, partly due to my
lack of enthusiasm for very early morning rising and
because I was studying botany, not music). The point is, the
university was known for its music, yet not once did I hear
jazz played or practised and my then-limited experience of
genres meant I did not seek it out.

George Melly was a magical discovery – along with Ian
Dury who had a love of jazz, and The Blockheads, whose
members included jazz-influenced musicians, and it was
this element of the music I picked up on. This music filled
a void I always had and tapped into the rebellious period of
my life because Dury and Melly were both characters who
did not conform. Further jazz findings like Albert Ayler,
Coltrane, Monk, Gustafsson and Brötzmann led me to the
music which truly spoke to my soul. How many others
found jazz later because they were not exposed to it when
they were young or it was just not on syllabuses, or they
thought of it as serious music for older people? Things have
moved on and jazz is an integral part of many schools'
music activities in the UK. It would be difficult now for a
student to play an instrument or sing without being
introduced to jazz and this is a great thing, but it will be a
little while before these young jazz lovers become adults
and really influence the UK scene.

It is still a widely held, even if unconscious, belief that
women should sing, play piano or play an orchestral
instrument, and these limited options at a young age might
go some way to explain why later on women feel excluded

from jazz – the 'masculine' instruments (bass clarinet, double bass and baritone saxophone, for example) being those which tend to solo more in jazz. Younger women have already been encouraged to choose orchestral instruments, which ensures they remain for the most part a component of a larger ensemble rather than a soloist.

A male trombone player who plays in jazz groups and classical orchestras gave further evidence when he said he believed the problems come much earlier on in school, maybe even pre-school. At a school where he teaches, he has had parents of girls who have chosen to study trombone suggest that girls "don't really play the trombone". When asked to explain, they say it is "quite a physical instrument and harder for girls to play". Even when he gently points out physical differences between boys and girls are really not that great, parents still prefer the girls play something else, something smaller.

Luckily, the musician concerned has the charm of a leprechaun and carries out gentle persuasion even though his blood, he says, "boils". He usually wins, meaning in the future there will be girls who have the opportunity to play brass.

Two teachers have given an interesting perspective too. Individual music lessons in school in the UK tend to be slotted into timetables because of the nature of a peripatetic teacher working a 9-5 day. So, students have to leave lessons which may be core subjects for GCSE (certificate of secondary education studies) or A-level studies. Parents encourage them to remain in class for maths, English and other core subjects rather than leave to have a music lesson. Girls are apparently far less likely to leave a lesson than boys. One parent explained that her daughter, while learning double bass, missed the same lesson (English) every week and had to work incredibly hard to catch up. She did and she also did really well with her double bass tests, but it was a difficult choice to make when exams were looming.

Taking risks – myths and veils

One factor which many people mention is that women are not as keen to 'take risks' as men. In terms of jazz this means they are less likely to take a solo, stretch out and take the lead in improvisation, especially in bebop with its fast, highly individual solo opportunities.

It is obvious that at youth and mature levels, women can take risks if given the opportunities. There is the chance to improvise in some classical compositions but these are few and far between. Jazz, on the other hand, is music which has an aural tradition and relies heavily on improvisation, so to play it well and be considered a superb musician you need to improvise. To develop and show your improvising skills, you need opportunity.

Improvising contains an element of risk-taking which can leave the performer more exposed but if a musician is well-schooled and gains experience, there is nothing to stop him or her from taking on solos. Women perhaps were not afforded the space to do so in early jazz but today their opportunities are greater.

In an encouraging environment, girls have been proved just as capable as boys when it comes to soloing or improvising. In the National Youth Jazz Orchestra there are female musicians on French horn, saxophone, baritone saxophone, flute, trombone, trumpet and vocals. The girls solo on the same level as the boys because they are encouraged to do so. Studies have shown that fewer women take solos in jazz orchestras than men, yet the quality of their work is the same.

The media

Until the last decade or so, jazz journalists, critics and authors were overwhelmingly male. This is changing and women have joined their ranks in the past few years.

However, a YouTube debate[18] was held recently between Jazzwise's Mike Flynn, vocalist and event organiser Georgia Mancio and pianists Aga Derlak from Poland and Sunna Gunnlaugs from Iceland which discussed women in jazz and one of the points they all agreed upon was the lack of female jazz writers still.

Historically, where jazz was concerned, the media presented women as weaker, musically impoverished and less able than men. Many male journalists have bullied female jazz musicians, belittling their talents and demeaning them. This is something which must change. Editors should call out reviewers who include little about the music in their reviews but much about the physical qualities of the female leads. They should encourage their critics to read about the women before they attend a gig just like they do for men. Know your musicians and their achievements. Know who the composers, arrangers and co-leads are, and write about them as equals. Not better or more, but equal. I have lost count of the number of times I

---

[18] https://www.youtube.com/watch?v=pkN0UcntnHE&feature=emb_logo with permission from Jazz Juniors Network at https://jazzjuniors.com.pl.

have been asked to advise women who have shown me reviews which border on sexist at best and downright misogynistic at worst. It is ridiculous that editors allow some reviews to pass and be published, particularly online. There are some great writers but they need to concentrate on the music rather than resisting change, which is coming whether they like it or not.

We have been fed the idea that jazz is for men ever since *jass* became jazz, well over 100 years ago. Sexist articles were not questioned by readers. The oft-cited editorial from a 1938 edition of DownBeat titled "Why Women Musicians Are Inferior" argued that women were "emotionally unstable" and "could never be consistent performers on a musical instrument" and other delightful imaginings. It was also mooted that women would never blow on brass or reeds for fear of looking unattractive and had neither the time, patience, ambition or economic motivation to woodshed (practicing techniques until you get them right). Further, women only had a few years' experience in jazz whereas men had far more history, and it was also suggested that piano and strings were "more suited to women".

Dr Brand reminds us, "Certainly musician authors like Gunther Schuller completely wrote women out of the history of jazz so historically there is very little written about women in jazz in the time jazz was evolving".

Not only are historical comments in some publications a remarkable display of ignorance about the presence of women in jazz but also they display a mind-boggling sense of entitlement. Yet we must not forget we are reading this with twenty-first century ideas and eyes. At the time of that article, DownBeat would have been largely written for men, by men and read by men. Nowadays editors have more than a male readership to please and, whilst the readership may be smaller, it is more mixed.

Whilst the press is considerably more affable towards female jazz musicians today and more writers are coming to know and report on good female musicians, there still remains, in certain journal quarters, a hangover from the days when sexism in the written word was acceptable.

Even in 1969 people were still trying to slow the hands of change. In spite of the number of successful jazz women, George T. Simon wrote in his book "The Big Band"[19], "Only God can make a tree...and only men can play good jazz".

Natt Hentoff was a long-term supporter of parity in jazz music and in 1952 he spoke out against journalists who described players as "the best female player [pianist, harpist, etc.]" implying she was good for a woman, women being of a lesser league of players than men. He believed that women should be judged using the same criteria as men. Acknowledging he himself had been discriminatory in the past, in a 1979 article Hentoff recalled, "When I was in my teens, I went with some friends to hear Woody Herman's band, and there, in the trumpet section, was a woman. We looked at Billie Rogers as if she had three heads and marvelled that she could even finish a chorus".

More recently the attitudes Hentoff observed and described over sixty years ago showed they are still present even on a subconscious level, when in the June 2012 issue

---

[19] Simon, George T. "The Big Bands", ISBN 0028724305. Publisher: Music Sales Ltd.

of DownBeat trumpeter Darren Barrett predicted that the twenty-two-year-old alto saxophonist Hailey Niswanger "has the power to be one of the best female alto saxophonists in the country, if not the world". Why not simply say "one of the best saxophonists"? (At 20, Niswanger took over the alto chair at Either/Orchestra in NYC whose occupants had included Miguel Zenón, Andrew D'Angelo and Godwin Louis, so clearly, it should have read "one of the best saxophonists".)

Journalists now are more careful and most editors take their responsibilities to ensure sexism is kept out of jazz reporting as much as possible. The media as a whole no longer re-enforces the idea that jazz is male-dominated but can – and often does – lead the way towards female recognition in jazz. It is a slow process because of the dinosaurs still occupying some editorial positions, but because it is a popular issue which has growing interest, many journals and papers are publishing articles about female musicians and giving them a good share of positive media coverage. For example, Clash Magazine recently published an article titled "Meet the Women Who Are Pushing UK Jazz Forward" and Culture Trip included three females in a 2016 article, "Ten Young British Jazz Musicians You Need to Know".

In 2017 The Financial Times published an article titled "British Jazz Gets a Blast of Female Energy" which foretold of changes afoot in gender balance and highlighted three female jazz musicians: Laura Jurd, Camilla George and Jazz Ahmed. Jazzwise published an interview with the Women in Jazz organisation in February 2020. UK female jazz musicians are definitely getting more press than pre-2000 and the way they are written about is respectful and reflects their talent rather than their body shape or scarcity. The media has a powerful role in who sees female jazz players and how they are portrayed, so this is a positive thing.

Many media reports of female-led festivals have been negative in the past, with journalists picking up on the fact that some bands billed as 'female' have male sidemen, and there is the association with feminism which sponsors may not want. The labelling of women as "female instrumentalists", some believe, led to the ghettoisation of women – putting them in one particular group and marginalising them.

There are several women-only festivals around the world but does a themed festival attract stereotypical expectations in the first place? Does it actually emphasise the differences between male and female performers? Could a precedent be set where events are divided according to gender?

It may do away with tokenism in the traditional sense but could it not be argued the male members of bands in women-only events are tokens too? Is it possible we shall ever simply not think of gender but just about the music?

When a woman first plays jazz, she is not thinking "I am a *female* jazz player" but sooner or later, some journalist is going to slap that label on her and she will carry it for the rest of her playing career. A man does not carry a label, he is just a jazz musician.

Reviewers will often point out "this is an all-girl band" or "a woman leads the ensemble", stating the obvious and highlighting the rarity of a woman leader. This kind of approach marks women as different or novel. They are not.

It also defines a musician by her gender, not her abilities or technique.

Adding a feminine description like *female jazz singer* or *female bandleader* immediately attaches a softer, less important note. Now, there is far more awareness and many journalists do not write about the gender of the band members they are reviewing because they are aware of the perception changing if they do. For example, Debbie Burke, who edited this book, is a jazz author and blogger from the US. When interviewing female jazz artists, she makes a practice of not pointing them out by gender but only speaking of them as musicians.

Examples of old-fashioned sexism can still be found, however. In a recent review, the male reviewer described the female singer (and composer) as "someone I have not heard of" and then described how she looked on stage. A little research (or a look at the programme he was given on arrival) would have informed him that she was nominated five times as a vocalist and won the Parliamentary Jazz Award for best album and composer. He was given a free CD of the concert and during the interval told her he did not know any of the songs (because they were originals perhaps?), preferred standards and might listen to the CD. He left after arguing with her about singers and jazz standards (which he would have preferred to hear a woman sing, apparently). Given he did not pay for his ticket or drink, he really should have done his research and concentrated on the music. A week later, the same journalist wrote a review of a male duo and the detail about their history, awards and past experience was notable. This is just one journalist who writes for just one online review column, but it is an example of how overt sexism can still be found in UK jazz.

Across the pond in America there is also a historical attitude which some journalists and writers may seem to perpetuate. An example of this is the following exchange which took place between writer Walter Kolosky, a US author, music journalist and co-host of the popular "Jazz Rocks Podcast" and myself. During research, the following quote was found from Kolosky's book "Girls Don't Like Real Jazz: A Jazz Patriot Speaks Out"[20]. It was intended as a humorous attempt to warn Americans about the impending loss of its rich musical history.

"The next time you are at a jazz show, check to see how many women are present. Then do a head count of how many women are there without a man. If you should find a woman alone, she is either the wife or girlfriend of one of the musicians or she has been stood up. Two women together are lesbians who think they like real jazz. I recently asked some women I knew why they didn't like jazz. Every single one, including my dear wife, responded that they absolutely loved jazz. In other words, they all lied".

Kolosky wrote the above in 2004. In 2020 he was asked if his views had changed with the following question: "In your opinion, is the reality that there are fewer women playing jazz and if so, what makes you believe that and do you have any theories as to why?"

His response both explained the context of his writing and his current views. "Many years ago, I wrote a tongue-

---

[20] Kolosky, Walter. "Girls Don't Like Real Jazz: A Jazz Patriot Speaks Out", ISBN 0976101602. Publisher: Abstract Logix.

in-cheek book [titled] 'Girls Don't Like Real Jazz'. It was a collection of short essays and stories, some true and some not, about the sad state of the jazz music scene in the United States. It was my humble effort to help save that business. The book took its title from one of those chapters. The main thrust of that essay was that women don't really like jazz. I surmised that those women who say they do enjoy jazz are jazz musicians themselves or married or dating one, and all the rest are liars. That has been my experience my whole jazz life. I still believe that".

He added that the quote was part of a satirical rant, probably misused in the paper I read, and that if read as part of the original book the line about two lesbians would hopefully make someone laugh; but out of context, he agrees the line "may not fare so well in today's climate".

I have to admit to feeling a sense of disappointment that he still believes women don't really like jazz or if they say they do, they are lying. Yet Kolosky acknowledges that in today's climate his comments would not go down well.

He tempered his comments: "Over my lifetime, I met about three women who I think were really into jazz, professional jazz musicians included. I wish it weren't that way. Please note, my 'they are all lying' was an attempt at humour. That is how I write. I know there are women who are fans. It is just a paucity".

Social media has a growing impact on the visibility of female jazz musicians. Many eminent musicians, male and female, have a strong presence on social media and this is because it provides a great platform to connect with their listeners and the people who buy their music. It also provides a network for musicians to connect and share opinions, discussions, other musicians they find and so on with each other. All those involved in the music – writers, photographers, record labels, producers and PR companies – have found that having a presence on social media can enhance visibility and there are many groups which support female musicians. Social media also provides a presence and exposure for funding bodies, initiatives and organizations which would otherwise find it difficult to reach a wide audience. Many women are doing great work on social media, making sure their music is exposed to listeners by uploading to platforms regularly and connecting with their audiences.

In reality, if you hear, for example, a jazz 'cello solo or an ensemble playing, do you have any idea about the people playing (other than if they are any good)? Do you know if they are male, female, non-binary, blond, brunette, fat, thin? Unlikely, so there is no typical 'female jazz' or 'male jazz', there is just jazz.

Lack of role models

The lack of women as role models in jazz continues to be an issue and something which many women and men talk about. If women do not see other women playing jazz, they will not be encouraged to join their ranks unless they are exceptionally strong-minded individuals. It also means there is less expectation of success for women because they see very few in a successful role.

Jack Hersh comments, "Lack of role models may have meant many younger women didn't feel inspired enough to enter the scene and many promoters may simply not have sought out female musicians for gigs".

For instrumentalists, more female role models would be welcome and also provide someone for women to talk to when sexism occurred.

Having female musicians playing as solo artists or as part of ensembles is important and relevant because in the same way that people are inspired by seeing people like them in successful positions, girls might watch a woman who is a successful jazz musician and think "that could be me". If they don't see women, where's their incentive?

Motherhood

One thing men cannot do that women can is bear children (yet, anyway). Motherhood does not come up very often in discussions but many females, whatever their career, choose to work less or not at all when they have children. Many take time out from their careers in order to bring up a family. It is personal choice and may depend on whether one has a supportive partner, if there are health issues either for the mother or baby (or both) – so many things – but overall, it is still often women who look after the children. I have known musicians whose children have been brought up going to gigs, staying up late, and for them, this is normal, but for many parents, life in the gigging world is not their choice for their children. Pregnancy brings with it risks and for some women this is an easy time, whilst for others the physical changes with pregnancy like nausea and dizziness can impact on the time a female can remain on stage.

Gender pay gaps

According to the National Office for Statistics (which obtains its figures largely from tax records through HMRC) currently, 50,000 people in the UK list their main occupational income as 'musician'. Of these 10,000 (20%) are women, and of those 207 (2.07%) are jazz musicians, 150 being soloists and 57 band members.

A recent survey of the music industry by Vick Bain (referenced in Chapter 3, Figure 12) showed that there is still a gender pay gap in the industry. The most recent figures available are for 2019 (before COVID-19 impacted the industry). It will be interesting to see how figures reflect in 2020 and whether the reduced revenues of music companies affect women more than men in terms of remuneration. For those performing it is difficult to obtain figures, but the difference in pay for women in companies involved with music publishing, promotion and other important aspects of the industry is pronounced, with women earning an average of 73p for every pound a man earns, which is 27% less than men. Regarding bonuses, 72% of women and 76% of men received bonuses but women received 77p for every pound a man received or 23% less. Only one company paid women more than men on average, with women receiving £1.10 for every £1 a man earned. Therefore, as a career option, the music industry is less attractive to women. This means fewer women will be in positions to promote, engage or champion female performers and given that jazz is less than 20% of all music performed and the number of women employed in these companies is under 37%, the chance of a female promoter handling a jazz artist is around 7%. That figure is also only true if all the females employed by a music company concentrated on promoting female jazz musicians (which they don't).

As stated above, it is more difficult to obtain figures for performers but research published in 2019 by HoneyBook[21], a management and invoicing platform used by freelancers, analysed over 350,000 invoices and found female musicians had earned only 38% of what their male colleagues had earned, the greatest pay gap of any of the professions. This was done in the US but no doubt if a study were carried out in the UK similar findings would be made. The surprising thing, though, is that as recently as 2017, male and female creatives, including musicians, did not realise they were not paid equally. Now they do, and women are far less likely to lower their prices knowing they are offered less than their male counterparts in almost every creative industry.

These are just some of the possible reasons for the lack of female jazz musicians in the UK. To these we can add other possible contributory factors, such as the fact women may not like being out late on a regular basis. Leaving a gig at 10 or 11 at night, travelling or walking back to the hotel or getting home by car is not a pleasant prospect. Many female performers have been followed, harassed and approached by intoxicated people as musicians leave later than the audience and often leave alone.

---

[21] https://www.honeybook.com/risingtide/2019–gender–pay–gap–report

There are several major reasons we are not seeing more women in UK jazz when considering the available research and experiences of many jazz professionals. To summarize:

- Lack of role models
- Unsocial hours and safety issues
- Motherhood
- Difficulty touring (women need different sleeping and bathroom arrangements)
- Isolation
- A lack of opportunities for female musicians
- Instrument choice
- Not associating jazz with career aspirations
- Negative connotations associated with being a female leader
- The perception of jazz being a 'male' interest by audiences, musicians and the media
- Gender pay gaps

It is clear that women are having to cope with difficulties in order to practice their profession which men may be unaware of. This book is not out to denigrate men but to ask certain questions: How many men feel subconsciously sexualised, ignored or side-lined? How many men have been paid less than a woman in the same band, or asked to dress in a particular way? How many men have no other men to mentor them, inspire them, or act as a role model? How many men have dealt with overt sexism or misandry? Yet, switch the question around and most women have come across some or all of these difficulties. In many respects, it is not the fault of one gender or another. It is simply entrenched beliefs and behaviours which have been accepted in jazz for decades.

Now that we understand the situation, we can do something about it. And there are those already pioneering ways to improve the visibility of women in UK jazz – which in turn will lead to a reduction in gender disparity. More on this later.

Claire Cope © Jake Walker

Kat Lee-Ryan of the Fabulous Red Diesel © John Sutton

Alina Bzhezhinska © Tatiana Gorilovsky

Juliet Kelly © Malcolm Sinclair

Abbie Finn © Malcolm Sinclair

Niki King © Marek Pieta Imagina Studio

Chapter 6

Forward

That change has already begun but needs to continue is clear but it needs to be permanent and lasting. Rapid changes which force quotas on every venue, festival or label may actually harm jazz in the long term. The art form in the UK finds itself at a fork it the road. Choose one way and it becomes increasingly distanced from its audience, remembered as a nostalgic music but with values which are not recognised as part of modern society. Take the other way, however, and jazz could become music which leads the way by accurately reflecting societal changes as it has always done and showing understanding of how people think and relate to the music around them.

If more change doesn't happen and is not publicized, people will have no idea how music can impact lives and no concept of how vibrant and culturally savvy UK jazz can be.

Expecting rapid change in deeply entrenched attitudes is perhaps unrealistic but we should be seeing more progress than we are – especially because the UK has made so many positive changes in other industries such as engineering, science and medicine; and also because there has been ongoing work in this field for many years which should have resulted in more change. It leads to an implication of deliberate and systemic misogyny, something which the jazz music industry gets accused of time and time again.

The Equality Act of 2010 forbids discrimination against all of the protected areas including:

- Age
- Disability
- Gender reassignment
- Marriage and civil partnership
- Pregnancy and maternity
- Race
- Religion or belief
- Sex
- Sexual orientation

Given all the protected areas, why do we still see clear gender disparity in jazz? Women are still more likely to be on the receiving end of sexism. When I have interviewed female musicians, this comes up regularly with no instigation and is still a thorn in the side of jazz music.

There needs to be a change in perception and it is this simple. View women as equal. Not threats, not lesser musicians, but equal; suited to playing any instrument they want to and to all parts of the jazz scene.

It has to be said also that a few women need to change their perceptions and expectations of themselves. Expect to lead a band if you want to, expect the slot at the festival.

It is apparent people want to see change in UK jazz. Many believe it is happening and there are seeds of hope scattered here and there, but they need a helping hand to take root, to germinate and grow. What many academics, innovators and panels want to believe is happening and what we actually witness are often different things. We want to believe in equality, and on race and other issues in jazz, this is certainly improving but clearly when it comes to gender, jazz in the UK has a long way to go. Those who are engaged in research, studies and projects about increasing the presence of female jazz musicians want to believe change is happening. Yet even with the energy and effort being put into it, the translation to the real world is incredibly slow.

There is agreement that women and men are equal in intellect, talent and ability. Women are progressing in technology, politics, research, education and many other areas but not in music and definitely not in jazz, which means the entire industry is losing a vital core of creativity, talent and business. What tools can we use in a positive way to bring about change?

Blind auditions

Blind auditions have been used in classical settings since the 1970s and have resulted in more female orchestra musicians. In a Guardian article titled "How Blind Auditions Help Orchestras to Eliminate Gender Bias" from October 2013, the writer comments that in the 1970s just 5% of players in classical orchestras were female, but by 2013 some had increased their percentage to up to 30%. Given that the size of orchestras and the number of players in each section remained stable, the only difference was initial auditions and sometimes auditions further down the selection pathway were held behind a screen. This meant that any gender bias – conscious or unconscious – was eliminated. Blind auditions have proven to increase numbers of films shown by female directors at film festivals too. Could this type of audition translate to jazz for musicians seeking grants, awards or a place in an ensemble?

Colleges and a different way of learning jazz

The Royal Academy of Music offered the first jazz degree course in the UK in 1986. Before then various institutions (the Royal Academy, Guildhall School of Music and Leeds College of Music) offered short courses, mostly postgraduate and one year in length, although at Leeds you could take a jazz and popular music course from 1965. Now several conservatoires and universities offer jazz degrees or jazz as an option within music degrees.

Before jazz studies were available, jazz musicians gained their education by experience and playing alongside other jazz musicians. Jam sessions, sitting in with established ensembles – these were how jazz musicians got their tuition in the past. Experienced musicians might sit in with newer ensembles. Davey Payne of the People Band once told me how John Surman sat in with them in one of their early sessions.

When I spoke to Steve Rubie of 606 Club in London, he said jazz was not allowed in music college when he attended in the 1970s. If students were caught playing jazz, they could be suspended – which of course made it a popular underground genre and probably encouraged more students to play it. Now, colleges realise the importance of improvised music and jazz, and the need to change the way students are prepared for the world of performing. Since the early 1990s the number of institutions offering jazz studies has increased exponentially. Some more recently introduced elements prepare musicians for the experience of performing in public and educate them in business practices. Whilst some would still argue that learning in any formalised manner goes against 'traditional' jazz practice, the value of a good, sound education in jazz is appreciated.

Diversity has to be part of any music genre today and colleges, universities and conservatoires in the UK are actively thinking now about how they invest in it. It is not enough to simply wait for the student demographic to reflect changes in society. It goes back to what was said earlier about jazz music itself being key to the process. Nick Reynolds, Head of Jazz at Chichester Conservatoire says, "I always feel that the music itself is the leveller since jazz from its beginnings embraced all these different styles and forms and continues to do so right up to the present day. So the ethos of the jazz department is founded on the idea that jazz is an inclusive and diverse art form. It celebrates diversity – so any student, no matter what musical background they come from, has an opportunity to tell their individual story through this music and all of the modules, jazz nights and workshops have this idea in mind. Equally jazz, due to its inherent evolutionary and wide-reaching embrace, includes all of these styles and individual voices within it.

"Establishing this ideal of inclusivity within diversity is no easy goal and has to be worked at on a day-to-day, semester-by-semester basis. But I have faith that jazz provides a powerful musical analogy for inclusivity and diversity and an experiential platform for allowing people the space to be able to have their voice heard within a community. That is what we are striving for in our department and every year we learn from the achievements and mistakes, student feedback, observations, research and most of all playing and jamming and being part of this community in order to develop this goal".

There are venues, including Vortex and 606 Club, which allow students to perform in front of an audience, thus providing the chance for them to see if they like this part of jazz or prefer another role. Many veteran musicians also provide opportunities for newly fledged jazz musicians to perform for a paying audience by allowing them to sit in or guest with them at a gig.

Colleges have also helped to improve confidence among female players who, though still in the minority, are being given more chances to play. Reynolds adds to his comments above saying, "With regard to the jazz studies at the Chichester Conservatoire, I have focused on the principle of inclusivity within the entire degree, ensuring that all students, no matter what their musical background, are part of a supportive community and that each student has the opportunity to develop their own voice within this music. Drop-in sessions and live jazz nights are open to any student wishing to participate at any level".

These small ensembles encourage men and women to play with and learn from each other, which means that from early on in their jazz studies, female and male musicians playing together becomes the norm. Young people expect to play with other young people, both male and female, and much of this attitude is because their education has provided them with the opportunity to do so. It allows women to become more confident in a jam session. If women do not actively engage in the jam session scene, they may miss out on valuable work opportunities as seen in Joy Ellis's work (noted earlier), and as a consequence they'd be further underrepresented in the wider jazz community.

When students are considering studying jazz, they will receive the opportunity to play with many different groups or solo formats, but before they audition for jazz studies, they need to have had the opportunity to reach the high standard required by the colleges and conservatoires. This is where summer schools and encouragement at high school level can make a difference, so support for young female jazz musicians is fundamental to youth jazz opportunities so they can achieve the level required. Joining a jazz course should be an option but one which male and females go into with their eyes open. They need the calling and they need to study hard. Ensuring provision is there so young musicians of all genders and races can be helped to reach a high enough standard where a jazz course is a viable option is a challenge. Keeping females interested in jazz in school is difficult because they do not have the same incentives as male students; they are in the minority and lack other females to discuss things with, learn from and be mentored by. Colleges will accept students who have reached the required standard regardless of gender so it is what happens in the earlier years that makes a difference to the numbers of women achieving the required standard and being accepted into jazz courses.

Women who are able to study jazz at university are incentivized to put into practice what they have learned, get back the money spent and not be side-lined.

For a while, higher learning might have to actively seek and perhaps discriminate for women. There could be women-only "taster" days which would allow women to get feedback from their peers and potential tutors on their readiness to audition for tertiary study, and offer constructive criticism if needed.

Institutions offering jazz studies could also conduct research into why more females do not study jazz, including social studies of the behaviour of teenage musicians, which might enable them to pinpoint when women leave jazz and the reasons for it. Looking from an adult perspective, it is easy to forget the awkwardness of youth. Could this not make the prospects of entering what is still a male-dominated arena more intimidating for teenage girls? How can it be made easier whilst losing nothing in terms of standards?

Youth jazz orchestras could be observed and the participants asked if they would like to study jazz at a higher level. Is there a way jazz can be studied further as part of a major in another subject altogether? Could more varied options be considered in degrees so students not opting for jazz as a major still have the chance to participate in jazz and opt in to more jazz units further in their studies? Could those studying jazz get more experience playing in front of audiences and tutoring in business management to prepare them for a career in jazz, making it a viable proposition?

It must also be remembered that outside of colleges and conservatoires, education in jazz is taking place through other routes. Many fine jazz musicians, male and female, have never had any college-based music training. They are not all youths either. Many musicians come to jazz as mature individuals, not wishing to go to college. A jazz degree is not the only route to success or of getting a jazz education.

Change

It is at the grassroots level where change is most likely to happen because it is here where attitudes change and understanding starts. In the 1970s and 1980s, successful women-only groups proved women could play jazz as well as men. Outside the UK there are several women-only platforms for jazz musicians including the Women in Jazz Festival in Sweden, The Palm Springs Women's Jazz Festival, Stockholm Women's International Jazz Festival, The Washington Women in Jazz Festival, The Sydney International Women's Jazz Festival and others. These spaces allow opportunities to network, perform and develop technical and artistic skills alongside supportive mentors and fellow musicians. All-female jazz groups are not a novelty. They have been part of the art form from the beginning. Traditionally, these groups provided opportunities to play and get experience and exposure.

Women-only events encourage them to share experiences and gain confidence on stage. Beyond that, they also help women to prove and understand for themselves, too, that not everyone matches the media's definition of *fit* when an article deigns to discuss women's appearance.

There needs to be a belief that women are there, available, willing and able to play. However, just as the grassroots level is where change happens, it is also where the sticking points are. Some people in the UK jazz scene feel uncomfortable with change. They like the status quo, which was never about equality. If the status quo was so good, there would be no issues with the societal changes that are happening. To delay or rebel against change, the women who speak out can find themselves tagged with labels like 'bossy', 'feminist' or other terms, and many women are uncomfortable with this. Even authors who write about women in jazz get labels attached to them by the male jazz community. They are 'feminist writers' or 'advocates for female musicians'. Most of them advocate for jazz full stop. Male musicians like the boy's club atmosphere of a jazz gig. Resistance to change at the grassroots level is a major obstacle to gender parity in jazz. It is difficult to see how to change it. Even if gender disparity is proven, how is it actually inequality? If there are not enough female jazz musicians to be found, how are organisers meant to fill programmes?

There are organisations offering support for female musicians including International Women in Jazz and Sisters in Jazz. In the UK we have women-only events including The Girl Plays Jazz and the She Is Jazz event which is part of the London Jazz Festival. There is the Birmingham-based Town Hall and Symphony Hall (THSH) Women in Jazz programme, and The National Youth Jazz Orchestra offers programmes tailored to encourage female musicians to go into jazz.

There are drawbacks to women-only groups, giving the impression of ghettoising women. Some see them as gentler and less experimental whilst others still view these groups as political. It feels like everyone has an opinion on female groups.

Most musicians want to be identified as musicians. Gender should have nothing to do with it.

Modern societal expectations and psychology

It is human nature to internalise negative comments and brush off positive ones. One negative comment in a review, for example, can spoil our perception of how a gig went even if it is surrounded by many positive ones. We need to switch this around, internalise the positives and act on these.

There have been other studies in gender imbalance in jazz; the facts discussed here are just a representation. Though there will be a small variation according to the demographics used in each study group, all of them make for revealing reading, showing overwhelmingly that gender discrimination is the reason for the disparity. Understanding and acknowledging this, we can now work to change it.

The power of youth

Jazz is enjoying a renaissance in the UK as younger people blend different genres of music, creating new kinds of jazz sounds. Young people see other young people playing jazz. Among these are female performers and there is no song and dance about it. They are simply there, part of the energetic and growing scene. It is these young people that are bringing real change. Changes in ideas, changes of attitude and importantly, a rejection of racism, sexism or any other 'ism'. A recent event at London's Jazz Cafe in Camden saw the performers, mostly young, deliver a salutary lecture to the audience right before they played on equality, youth initiatives and how everyone had equal rights. It was empowering for them and mostly, (apart from a gentleman who told anyone who would listen *how entitled these young people were today!*) the audience took it well. It is these young people who will both demand and initiate change and who hopefully will see the day dawn – maybe when they themselves are middle-aged and watching a new generation of jazz musicians – when being female will no longer be an issue. It will be just about who can play the music.

Musicians talk of a revival in the small club arena and the diversity of the music on offer. That diversity includes interesting female jazz musicians. As cafés, small venues and bars turn their commercial minds to a wider clientele, the jazz scene is more diverse than ever. Venues like Steam Down in Deptford have chosen to follow a more eclectic music route which means audiences get to see acts whose potential otherwise may never have reached the stage.

Away from London, venues across the UK such as Jazz at the Albert in Bedminster, Bristol, and Manchester's Band on the Wall offer opportunities to musicians. Snape Maltings in Suffolk, traditionally a home for classical music, is more open to jazz, encouraged by the packed auditorium when players like Pee Wee Ellis, Julian Joseph, Courtney Pine, Barb Jungr and Claire Martin perform. Fleece Jazz Club and Ipswich Jazz Club showcase new talent alongside major players. Leeds has many venues willing to support music in all its diversity including The

Wardrobe, Sela Bar and Smokestack. Even through COVID-19, jazz musicians have continued to perform and be watched via the ever-inventive use of technology (like streaming). The jazz scene has come back to life with a vengeance; and women are part of it. Much is down to the nature of the audiences.

There are initiatives attracting young people like Jazz Warriors and Jazz re:freshed, there are places for young people to play and the veterans are encouraging a new generation. We see Evan Parker playing alongside Moses Boyd, veteran sax player Davey Payne alongside Hannah Marshall at Cafe OTO, and many other examples of the older generation encouraging younger players.

Dr Hingwan of Vortex Jazz Club agrees younger musicians change the audience's perceptions when she says, "The Vortex can be a very male-dominated space for some of the gigs. Gigs with younger musicians tend to be a little more balanced. The Shape of Jazz to Come series I curate with Dave Holland [double bass player] has a very balanced audience in terms of gender, but that's because the usual Vortex audience[s] don't come".

On attitudes within the industry, Faye Patton believes younger musicians are far more relaxed about gender. "Male musicians", she says, "have been brought up in the past to be allowed to make mistakes and not feel self-conscious about it whereas for women it was harder because men expected them to be bad in the first place or be amazing because they had 'made it' to the band".

One lovely thing which happens regularly is that younger people don't call jazz a 'scene' in the UK anymore. They call it 'family' or their 'community'. They are taking ownership, the women are there as equals and the future is looking more and more like a place where those who play it will be gender-blind, colour-blind and simply listening for great music.

The musicians coming onto the jazz circuit in the UK have helped breathe new life into the scene. Women are visible in this younger demographic and include musicians such as Laura Jurd, Zara McFarlane, Polly Gibbons, Nubya Garcia, Yazz Ahmed, Poppy Ajudha and Ali Affleck alongside their male counterparts like Elliot Galvin, Sam Leak, Kit Downes and Reuben Fowler. There are different styles and a blend with high quality street music which has brought jazz to a wider audience. Jazz venues now might be the traditional ones such as Ronnie Scott's, 606 Club and Pizza Express, to name a few, a small-to-medium venue like Cafe OTO, Oliver's Jazz Bar, Iklectic Art Lab and Vortex or even a pop-up café venue. Jazz is everywhere and it is the young musicians who bring with them a total disregard of old-fashioned prejudices and gender discrimination. To them, a woman can play anything and it is her choice whom she plays with, what she plays and when. Put the young people in charge of programmes and rosters and we might get to gender parity far sooner than we had hoped.

Before COVID-19 small and mid-sized venues were opening or re-opening across the UK. Examples include Luna Lounge in Leytonstone, The Forge in Camden, Hideaway in Streatham, Pizza Express Jazz Club on Dean Street and Kings Place in King's Cross. Only time will tell whether the crisis sees people return in numbers but it feels encouraging.

Positive initiatives

There are other positive initiatives for women in UK jazz too. One is Cafemnee, a supportive organisation for women set up by saxophone player Millicent Stephenson. As a musician Stephenson realised five years ago that she had met very few other female jazz saxophonists and hardly any keyboard players or drummers. A quick survey of other musicians found they felt the same – where were the women? Cafemnee held its initial meeting with just a few in attendance but the group has grown. Five years on they now hold workshops, host art and music events, and address topics such as how to mentally approach performing, how to cope with the pressure of a jam session – something Stephenson found the women particularly nervous about – and how to grow as a musician. From Cafemnee has come working groups and solo performers with a network of supportive musicians behind them. Stephenson also runs online workshops and events where women can share experiences and offer support to each other.

The progress towards gender parity has been frustratingly slow for decades. It is bizarre how slow jazz has been to catch on to changes in attitude and the rise of female equality. However, there are some organisations which offer more than discussion and have undoubtedly helped increase the visibility of women in UK jazz. They include:

- Help Musicians UK – HMUK launched its pilot programme, Jazz Promoters Fellowship, in 2017 based on research which revealed the underrepresentation of women in UK jazz. HMUK looks to create a more diverse and inclusive jazz scene in the UK by helping male and female promoters establish themselves regionally and nationally, and to acknowledge the jazz scene's gender imbalance through exploration into why it exists and how we can work together to redress it. During the COVID crisis HMUK supported musicians who faced difficulties and is now working to help them re-emerge post-pandemic.

- Women Make Music – Set up by PRS after discussions in 2010 revealed the disparity in UK music, including jazz. Their aims are:

  i) To break down assumptions and stereotypes within the music industry by encouraging role models for future generations;

  ii) To raise awareness of the gender gap and to ensure that women are aware that support for new music is available to them;

  iii) To increase the profile of women, trans and non-binary artists who are creating new music in the UK;

  iv) To encourage women, trans and non-binary artists who may otherwise not have applied for PRS Foundation funding to do so. They have funded and supported many jazz artists with projects including Poppy Ajudha and Cassie Kinoshi's SEED Ensemble.

- Blow the Fuse (BTF) – Winners of the Parliamentary Jazz Awards Service to Jazz 2020, BTF was formed in 1989 by musicians and composers Deirdre Cartwright and Alison Rayner. It plays a crucial role in raising awareness about women jazz musicians and offers support and opportunities to perform. It also runs club nights at the Vortex Jazz Club and other venues, manages UK jazz tours with new musical works, innovative collaborations and educational projects, and has produced 14 albums on Blow the Fuse Records to date. BTF has contributed to raising the profile of women jazz musicians, including young and emerging artists, through their innovative project "Tomorrow the Moon". Since 2012, these seasons of double-bills of new jazz music performed by women-led projects in London have featured groups led by Laura Jurd, Yazz Ahmed, Diane McLoughlin, Carol Grimes, Shirley Tetteh, Lauren Kinsella, Annie Whitehead, Roz Harding, Nikki Iles, Chelsea Carmichael, Camilla George, Nubya Garcia, Alison Rayner and Deirdre Cartwright.

- London East Jazz Network –Works to increase awareness of jazz music and get rid of discrimination in jazz. It describes itself as 'creating bridges through the excitement of jazz'.

- Women in Jazz (WIJ) – Founded by Louise Paley and Nina Fine to champion female jazz musicians as performers, festival producers and managers.

Among other professional roles, WIJ women build
visible careers in all areas of jazz. WIJ curates
events from radio shows, workshops, festival work
and video events. It has a strong online community
with over 7000 members, and its educational
workshops are open to both men and women
because everyone needs to be involved. It also
supports mentorship programmes so young women
feel confident to pursue a career in jazz in any role.
WIJ is hoping to see a growth in the number of
young women pursuing a creative career in jazz and
the music industry as they seek to increase the
numbers of role models for female musicians.

- Ronnie Scott's Charitable Foundation – Supports
  projects to encourage female jazz musicians. For
  example, in 2019 Jazz North was awarded a grant
  of £5,130 to develop and deliver Jazz Camp for
  Girls, a series of one-day intensive workshops for
  girls 9-13 years old to address the gender imbalance
  in jazz.

- The Girl Plays Jazz Project – Dedicated to
  supporting and promoting girls and young women
  in jazz. It offers one-day workshops to introduce
  girls to jazz, blues, funk and world music
  improvisation, and to develop girls and young
  women as jazz musicians. The girls can play with
  top-quality acts that host master classes. Acts have
  included a Cuban big band workshop led by Sara
  McGuiness and Jimmy Hernandez, a samba
  workshop led by the Brazilian drummer Cyro Zuzi,

a gypsy jazz day led by La Bouche Manouche featuring Irene Serra, and a free jazz and improvised music masterclass with Shirley Smart and Charlotte Keeffe. The project also seeks performance and development opportunities for girls, and in 2019 performed at Ronnie Scott's Jazz Club and the European Bank of Reconstruction and Development's Policy Awards. Visits to recording studios and other events give girls an opportunity to experience different parts of the music industry.

- Tomorrow's Warriors – Supports any individual likely to have barriers in the way of their career progression, especially BAME people and females. A recent evolution of Tomorrow's Warriors is the setting up of girls' bands in order to encourage more female musicians. This experience gives them the chance to avoid the over-competitive atmosphere of the mixed and male bands, and provides encouragement for them to continue in jazz. More girls are reaching the standard expected for entry into conservatoires and several have now been accepted into jazz courses. Success stories include Shirley Tetteh and others. Tomorrow's Warrior also has a Female Frontline Ensemble which is a collective of nine female musicians with the aim to improve visibility.

- Jazz re:freshed has a weekly Thursday showcase at the Mau Mau Bar in London's Notting Hill. It was formed in 2003 to provide alternative performance opportunities for young, mostly black UK jazz artists who felt disenfranchised by London's mainstream jazz scene, and dovetails with Tomorrow's Warriors which concentrates on teaching jazz whilst **Jazz re:freshed** provides the space for musicians to play.

- There are also podcasts such as Millicent Stephenson's "Success Beyond the Score" to help people navigate their way through the music industry.

In addition to the above, funding projects are available for jazz music like the Arts Council England grants for music. The website states, "From 13 May 2019 until 31 March 2021 we are making an additional ring-fenced budget of £1.5 million available within National Lottery Project Grants specifically to support the grassroots music sector", and adds that "grassroots music venues and promoters are vital to England's music ecology, developing music and audiences as well as supporting talent development". Arts Council England makes funding available to those whose main function is to host and/or promote live music events in venues, and explains, "We are also keen to support projects that develop diverse approaches to music programming, incorporating for example classical, jazz, folk, and/or world music alongside contemporary pop". Projects include live music programming as well as activities that put live music venues and promoters in a better position to deliver their work in the long term such as purchasing essential equipment, carrying out building work, developing new routes into off-stage roles and business planning.

The Performing Rights Society (PRS)[22] offers support for showcases of new jazz musicians. Another source, Youth Music, supports and nurtures young musicians whose access to music is limited due to where they live or their current hardship.

There is also the Jerwood Foundation which funds numerous projects and has supported arts in the UK over more than 30 years including private sponsorship and corporate investment in festivals.

Jazz North offers grants for the arts which includes funding for jazz projects, and there are charitable support programmes and grants offered by organisations such as the Peter Whittingham Jazz Award and Jazz South which help those who are having trouble finding the right resources.

Whilst this book is not a study of funding, there is money available, often hidden deep within organisations, so it is worth searching. It is difficult to obtain precise figures because the size and number of grants vary from year to year.

What is clear is that this support remains invaluable. Trumpet player Charlotte Keeffe tells how important receiving an award from HMUK was in showing her she was seen, heard and felt; that she was important enough on the UK scene to receive an award in spite of being a lone female in a predominantly male world. Keeffe recalls, "HMUK awarded me with a Postgraduate Award, which was a real confidence booster and a big support during my studies at The Guildhall School of Music and Drama in London. I was the only woman in my year group whose

---

[22] Performing Rights Society https://prsfoundation.com

principal study was an instrument. During my time as a student, I couldn't wait to embrace more of the jazz scene in London. I took myself to all sorts of jam sessions and was very often faced by a wall of white, male saxophonists and guitarists doing their thing relentlessly 'blowing' all over each other. This might sound like I'm referring to what it was like years ago but this was the case for me only a few years ago and even in legendary jazz clubs like Ronnie Scott's!

"I quickly believed I was not being seen or heard in these environments but receiving this award really gave me the confidence I needed by reminding me that I am! It's so important that charities like HMUK support and promote female jazz musicians as it paves the way to more inclusivity and equality in music and the arts".

The UK is also included in studies and work carried out by the European Jazz Network (EJN), a working group of experts who have, as a result of analysis and studies of the jazz scene, developed programmes aimed at working with concert organizers, promoters and producers to give them all the information to put norm-criticism into practice, ending discrimination on any criteria, and to implement this in their organizational structure as it pertains to booking, arranging concerts, communication and marketing.

EJN members adopted a new manifesto at the 5th European Jazz Conference in August 2018 and committed to embracing gender balance in the jazz sector and creative music. It was one of the outcomes of a four-year programme that examined diversity and discrimination in the jazz sector and had financial support from the Creative Programme of the European Union. The manifesto resulted

from a detailed consultation and discussion process that
started with a working group of members at the European
Jazz Conference 2017 in Ljubljana and continued
throughout the year through virtual meetings and a face-to-
face seminar at the Gateshead International Jazz Festival at
Sage Gateshead in April 2018.

The Manifesto underlines what EJN members,
representing festivals, venues, clubs and national/regional
support organisations in 35 countries, now pledge to do.
More details can be found on their website
(www.europejazz.net/ejn-manifesto) but this is an
important agreement, alongside Keychange (see below),
targeted towards jazz and creative music. It represents
concrete steps in terms of addressing the issue of gender
balance, with the awareness that a shared effort between
creators, presenters and educators is needed in order to
change the status quo.

The pledge, to which over 90 organisations in Europe
including the UK signed up, includes considering how
gender balance is addressed in work; and collaboratively
seeks solutions to learn from each other's experiences. The
pledge is found through the EJN page above.

Other initiatives not specialising in jazz but nonetheless
important in raising the profile of women in music are
growing in number. 100 % HER is a collaboration between
Universal Production Music and SHESAID.SO with
support from SHE IS THE MUSIC. The collaboration,
which launched in 2019, offers a platform for music by
women and gender minorities so their voices can be heard.
Artists were invited to submit music to be considered for an
album titled "100% Her". Of the 470 global submissions,

they selected ten for the album which was released during the 2019 International Women's Day celebrations. All tracks were composed, mastered and mixed by women. They are now in the midst of producing a second "100% HER" album for release in 2021.

SHE IS THE MUSIC is a global, independent and unifying organisation for women that offers support for female-based initiatives. SHESAID.SO is an international network of women working in music and began in London in 2014 under the leadership of Andreea Magdalina. There are over 12,000 members with chapters in London, Los Angeles, France, Germany, South Africa and other worldwide locations. Though not specific to jazz, these entities are important for raising the profile of females in the music industry in all roles and at all levels. More can be found on their websites listed in the resources section.

Deirdre Cartwright(L) and Alison Rayner at Kings Place
© Jane C. Reid

Charlotte Keeffe © Sean Cullum

Georgia Mancio © Peter Fairman

Kim Cypher © Ron Milsom

Tamar Osborn © Steve Thompson

Shirley Smart © Monika Jakubowska

Rosie Frater-Taylor © Phil Barnes

Chapter 7

The Journey Towards Change

In the UK the dearth of women in jazz is confusing; not so much the low numbers in the last century, given the history of jazz, but that the change has not come in spite of there being many people working for years in this area. Not many art forms can excuse themselves by saying they discriminate because of historical attitudes. Change should have come sooner to jazz and some worry that it will become so out of touch it is no longer relevant.

However, hope springs eternal. Some areas of jazz are slowly opening up to more female performers. There is a sense that we are on the cusp of change; a shambling, inching towards change, but it is happening.

As far back as 1989 there was realisation that more than commentary was needed. In Luton, a town in Bedfordshire, an arts centre obtained funding and developed a record label with increasing the presence of female artists in jazz, fundamental to its philosophy. The label, 33 RPM, released its first albums in 1989 featuring soul singer Sister Rose and bass player/vocalist Cuttie Williams. The logic behind the focus on female musicians was the realisation that many female jazz artists were being ignored by male-dominated clubs and labels. When it came to selling CDs at gigs – an important part of the musicians' income – women often did not have any, in spite of being amongst the best performers. So this small label, streets ahead of the rest at the time, decided to concentrate on female musicians. Now under the direction of Executive Producer Paul Jolly, the label (which changed its name to 33Jazz) continues to advocate for female performers and over a third of their releases are by female performers including Tina May – considered one of Europe's premier jazz vocalists – pianists Andrea Vicari and Kate Williams, saxophonists Clare Hirst and Karen Sharp, and singers Estelle Kokot, Maggie Nicols, Joanna Eden, Louise Gibbs and Anita Wardell. As well as UK artists, the label's releases have included international stars such as American vocalists Deborah Brown, Leslie Paula, Shaynee Rainbolt and Joan Viskant, and Italian bassist Silvia Bolognesi (now working with the Art Ensemble of Chicago). The label's list of female artists is impressive and growing. Recent acts have included Kitty LaRoar, Gg, Jayne Mason, Jo Schwartz, Shirley Smart, Beverley Beirne and many others. Jolly is involved with the UK jazz scene as a reedsman and has been part of many events which promote UK jazz such as the London Jazz Platform in 2017 which showcased 14 acts. Having a label so actively involved in the UK jazz scene and visibly supporting female artists is a boon to the industry.

Event organisers are also navigating the tricky position of trying to include more female musicians whilst avoiding tokenism. Guitar player and stalwart of the UK jazz scene, John Russell, organises the popular Mopomoso concert series events at London's Vortex Jazz Club and co-runs the Weekertoft record label. He believes Mopomoso benefits from the presence of female performers and members of the audience. Including females on every programme influences how the music is perceived. He also comments that the scene is strengthened because there are many good female players.

Most event organisers today support good jazz music and whoever brings the talent regardless of gender. However, there are still men keeping the flag of sexism raised. Recently I had a PR manager email me, asking me to review one of his artists. I had reviewed for his company before – for free – and this time I declined because I can only take on so much free work if I am to review properly and the music was not, in my opinion, very good (I didn't tell him that). The PR manager replied by saying that I only wrote about free jazz, never reviewed the music he sent me and that I clearly hated men. Not only are his first two statements untrue but how does not wanting to work (again) for free make me hate men? A sexist comment was the only weapon he actually had. How does he think this makes me want to review for his company again?

It still takes a very brave woman to put herself up for the scrutiny and judgement which voicing a complaint may bring, but unless we challenge poor behaviour by anyone, not just men, how can we embrace and enable the change which must come?

And it is coming. The #MeToo initiative gave many women the courage to come forward and name and shame bullies. #MeToo saw support from celebrities, TV and social media, and precipitated a flurry of stories highlighting the deplorable liberties some men of influence have taken over women. That momentum has continued and spread into almost every industry.

Jazz has proved itself far from innocent or scandal-free. In the autumn of 2017, across the Atlantic, the Boston

Globe reported[23] that over a period of thirteen years, the Berklee College of Music – one of the premier training grounds for jazz musicians – quietly let eleven faculty members go after students reported sexual harassment. The #MeToo initiative revealed that sexual harassment is still alive and well in the creative industries, including jazz. It gave women the confidence to share what happened to them and the number of women was surprising and also disappointing, not because they came forward but because there were so many. However, some men still had a problem with accepting the truth. I interviewed several women about this and wrote a piece for a major online column. The editor said he was pleased to publish it, and he did, but then added the caveat of an op ed which meant the views expressed were not those of the editor. Later, the article was removed from the site, showing that some male publishers and editors are not yet brave enough to support articles which highlight sexism in jazz.

The #MeToo initiative inspired the We Have Voice Collective which has as its code of conduct the promotion of safer workplaces in the performing arts. By workplaces they include the stage, dressing rooms, offices, studios – anywhere performers need to work. It is led by 14 American-based women and institutions can sign up to the pledge. Currently 61 institutions have embraced the code of conduct and whilst most are US institutions there are those from Italy and Canada too. Eventually, it will be worldwide

---

[23] "Berklee College Alleges Sexual Abuse"
https://www.bostonglobe.com/metro/2017/11/08/berklee–college–lets–teachers–quietly–leave–after–alleged–sexual–abuse–students–least–one–found–another–teaching job/yfCkCCmdJzxkiEgrQK4cWM/story.html

and include the UK. In addition, over 1200 jazz influencers have signed the open letter which outlines their aims.

Compared to the rest of the world the UK is not doing too badly in terms of inventive organisations that tackle gender disparity. It is important to use them and put the available support into action. America has many initiatives on national and local levels which work to increase the prevalence of women in jazz. Just a few examples include the University of North Texas's (UNT) Women in Jazz Initiative, which is a student government organization for the women and non-binary students in UNT's jazz program. The initiative strives to create a welcoming environment for all women and non-binary people in UNT's jazz department. There is also the Berklee Institute of Jazz and Gender Justice founded by Terri Lyne Carrington. In Germany, Jazzfest Bonn has discussed gender disparity and the festival committee has vowed to tackle the numbers of men hugely outweighing the women.

The good news is these organisations are here and provide mentoring, role models and other people to share experiences with and learn from. The bad news is they are still needed. However, jazz is such an international phenomenon that initiatives which work in one place have a habit of being adopted elsewhere as musicians share their experiences and values. Each organisation that embraces the cause is important in instigating change both in the UK and worldwide.

The Keychange initiative started in 2017 as a European talent development programme. An ambitious project, it describes itself as "a pioneering international initiative which transforms the future of music whilst encouraging festivals and music organisations to achieve a 50:50 gender balance by 2022. Keychange aims to accelerate change and create a better, more inclusive music industry for present and future generations".

Keychange has support from the PRS Foundation and Musikcentrum Öst, the Creative Europe Programme of the European Union, and makes no secret of its desire to completely restructure the music industry in order to create a gender-equal platform. It has partners in 12 countries and encourages organisations to sign up and advocate change in proactive ways through partners, ambassadors and programmes.

A look at the sign-up figures for organisations pledging their support – to reach a 50:50 participation by 2022 – sees the UK with a far larger number of organisations signed up than other countries. Whilst it is important to note that Keychange covers all music genres, it is relevant because change is needed across all genres (see link in references section). The 50:50 goal will be reached when half the programmed acts include at least one woman/transgender/non-binary person. Some of the participating festivals are going further than this, but Keychange wants this first target to be achievable and encourages everyone involved to be thinking about long-term change. Given the UK has 127 festivals and organisations signed up, might we expect to have seen more change over the last three years? A chart from June 2020 showing the numbers of participating entities follows below.

Fig 15. Numbers of organisations per country signed up to Keychange

Country	Number of festivals and organisations signed up to Keychange
UK	127
Canada	22
Germany	19
United States	11
Australia	10
Spain	10
Sweden	9
Norway	7
France	7
Netherlands	5
Switzerland	5
Brazil	5
Finland	3
Poland	3
Portugal	3
Belgium	2
Austria	2
Turkey	2
Greenland	2
Iceland	2
Estonia	2
Italy	2
Denmark	2
Hong Kong	1
China	1
South Korea	1
Hungary	1
Ukraine	1

Colombia	1
Thailand	1
Czech Republic	1
Malta	1
Slovenia	1
Afghanistan	1
Romania	1
New Zealand	1
Ireland	1
Worldwide Organisations	7

Given the large number of UK organisations which have pledged for 50:50 representation, the obvious question is why are we still so far away from the goal? Why is the UK not leading the way? According to PRS figures, things look to be moving forward slowly. For instance, from 2011-2019 the number of female musicians increased from 14% to 19% – a 5% increase over eight years. At that pace it will be at least 2060 by the time we see the UK approaching 50:50 representation.

Actions like signing up for Keychange may not feel as if they have radical effects and, perhaps for jazz at least, parity by 2022 is far too ambitious, but they do provide impetus for different parts of the industry to look closer at themselves. For example, Leeds College of Music signed up to Keychange and pledged to try to maintain a 50:50 gender balance in their annual Sounds Like This Festival which showcases new and experimental music.

There is a degree of credibility for festivals and colleges which achieve their pledge to Keychange. In 2019, for example, Marsden Jazz Festival achieved 50:50 gender equality after signing up to Keychange only the preceding April. Although the pledge was to achieve parity by 2022, the festival organisers rose to the task and immediately put on a programme featuring 50:50 male-to-female performers. Their artistic director is quoted in the press as saying, "Jazz and improvised music is a living art form, so it makes total sense that our programme should reflect society as a whole. We are proud to champion some incredible female artists and help inspire the next generation". By achieving the goals, they gained positive publicity for the festival and demonstrated it is a place where everyone is welcome. The organisers of Marsden Jazz Festival were even prouder when they checked acts in their past programmes and found they had achieved parity before, in 2018, taking into account the guidelines of Keychange (where 50% of the gigs programmed should have at least one female/non-binary/transgender artist). Interestingly, the Marsden staff members also looked at their audience figures and realised they had achieved a roughly 50:50 gender balance there as well, indicating that audience attendance demographics are related to programming. For the future they are going to make sure that they have at least 50% of the gigs they programme led by a female/transgender/non-identifying artist.

The Marsden organizers state in the media that although they are proud to have achieved parity and lead in some areas, they realise that in others they will need to be led and learn from their partners and artists. Surely this is how a successful jazz festival continues to engage with its audience and artists!

Many other festivals in the UK including the Cheltenham Jazz Festival, EFG London Jazz Festival, Glasgow International Jazz Festival, Hull Jazz Festival and Manchester Jazz Festival are among those signed up to Keychange. Given the disparity in male and female acts they have their work cut out, but the goals are clear and the energy and determination are there.

A significant impact of having more women in jazz – or any creative industry – is that it allows more choices for everyone because there are more people to take on different roles. Men or women can be leaders, in the spotlight, power up initiatives or opt to be in the background, part of the team and taking a supportive role. Some female musicians are supported by their partners who take pictures, arrange the gigs, transport, or provide food, PR, child care and such. One guy even said he managed himself out of his wife's band because he spent so long organising things that he no longer had the time to practice, but it was his choice. Equally, there are supportive women; wives and partners who choose to be the support and make life easier so their partners can perform or be in the studio. Having everybody on equal terms provides flexibility and imparts empowerment across the board.

Tokenism – the inclusion of women to make up quotas rather than because of their talents – is becoming a thing of the past and women are being accepted as equals. One older musician told me, "Well, we are getting used to things being different. It used to be I spoke to men all the time but now the person arranging a gig is a woman, the person organising my pay and even my driver might be a woman". In some instances perhaps there is just not a big enough pool of female musicians to select from. UK jazz may take a while but it will get there. It has to.

If festivals and venues need to actively discriminate for women over men to fill quotas does that mean there are a few female musicians with packed diaries whilst the men fight for the 50% remaining work, and there are more men so each one will get less work? Are men soon going to have to start campaigning for men's rights due to parity issues?

Many UK jazz musicians are discomfited by the fact we are even having to think of anything other than the music. How did we get to a place where anyone felt uncomfortable in jazz? Why wasn't it more equal from the start?

At the end of all this, it would be great to believe there will be a time when all the initiatives for women in jazz will be redundant. Because finally, gender will not be an issue.

Music is vulnerable to labels like any industry and jazz is fighting to shed the sexist label it has gained. Sexist behaviour is generally called out today and it means there is more respect for women and a wariness of ignoring them.

Potential problems with sudden parity

If I had the power to change things I would not make it 50:50 men and women in jazz overnight. This may sound as if I am not supporting change but that's not the case. I want to look ahead to a time when gender is not part of the criteria for selecting a jazz musician but also when the pool to choose from is vast enough and has enough women in it that the likelihood for an even split can be achieved organically.

There is increasing pressure to force change to happen quickly. However, because jazz is so male-dominated, it might be smart to take a firm but steady rate of change. Introducing absolute instant parity would mean putting a formula on an art form and 50:50 then becomes a quota, and if reached, it would mean men and women might lose out simply because they were one too many of their gender. This does not sit well in any art form.

Understanding the disparity and accepting it as fact is one thing. Doing something about it is another. It is easy to point to initiatives and articles, papers and changes, and decide that there is little to be done. There is an attitude of "change is happening and if it is slow, well, it is slow but we'll get there". Not good enough. In the slow meantime many women are losing their place in jazz, some leaving the industry because of the lack of encouragement or opportunity; the music is losing a creative core. A goal of 50:50 by 2022 suggested by Keychange is most definitely a positive move but artists want to be chosen for their merit, not simply because the programmer has to fill a quota. The fluidity inherent in free art must be reflected in the free choice of players.

Fulfilling a quota feels like papering over the cracks and giving yourself a pat on the back for being diverse. It doesn't resolve the underlying issues.

Also, if suddenly the missing volume of women (and we are not talking small numbers here but a whopping 40-plus percent in many areas) were miraculously put on stage, who would they have as role models? Who will they learn from and who will mentor them? Would they all rely on the 5-10% already there? More likely, they would rely on the males who currently dominate the UK scene, so female musicians would become reliant upon the support of their male counterparts. For men, there are usually male mentors; for women, not so many. How do we put in place change which is permanent without stipulating precise quotas and formulaic programming?

Some of the answers have to be found by upping the profile of women in UK jazz. Let women promote events, let them participate more in events and start female mentoring programmes for females. Right from the start when a woman picks up an instrument – whatever kind that is – don't put a gender on her choice.

Kitty LaRoar (c) Robert Crowley

Yazz Ahmed © Seb JJ Peters

Millicent Stephenson © Keri Hunt

Flo Moore with Alex Webb © Monika Jakubowska

The "F-List"

Wouldn't it be amazing if, instead of programmers bemoaning the scarcity of female musicians, there was somewhere a list, a register which contained female musicians, what they played, the genres they played? Well, now such a list exists. Called the F-List, it was instigated by Vick Bain who says, "For those scratching their heads over the fact they don't know any female artists I have compiled a snapshot of over 300 UK labels in different genres. Collectively these labels have over 3K signed female[24] artists on their rosters and some of these labels will have international artists; as long as they are signed to a UK label, I will include them".

The list is invaluable to venue promoters, curators and festival directors as well as writers and journalists.[25]

The F-List was designed to be the most up-to-date, comprehensive directory of female UK musicians and it facilitates those looking for profiles and professional opportunities for them. The vision is for women to more successfully start and sustain a career in the music industry. Those seeking musicians can search by genre, area or name, and musicians can list themselves for free. The F-List aims to contain details of every female artist signed to a record label or releasing music independently in the UK and it already has over 2000 singers and bands (and for jazz, there are over 300 women solo artists, bandleaders or members of ensembles).

---

[24] *Female* in the F-List refers to cis female, trans female or those living solely as a female, or those who identify as binary or gender fluid.

[25] The F-List https://vbain.co.uk/the–f–list https://smarturl.it/the–f–list

With this resource freely available, there is no reason for people to say it is hard to find female musicians. Bain has basically done the work for them. The list will be continually updated with details of solo artists and groups with at least one female member, and covers every genre from rock and pop to jazz and classical, and includes songwriters and composers.

The F-List is poised to become a resource for the whole music industry and a huge boon to jazz women. It will also prove a very useful tool for journalists, photographers, reviewers and those wishing to contact these women because it lists their websites as well. No excuse not to write about women, see women and hear them perform.

The list, as Bain herself says, is not definitive. There are women who are not yet on the list and should be, but the list will grow.

Chapter 8

Into the Future

So how do people view the future of gender disparity in UK jazz?

Jack Hersh of Jazz Cafe, Camden, says, "These days, you'd say there was still an imbalance but it is improving. We pick our artists based on talent alone, and we're finding many more of our jazz musicians, particularly the younger generation, are female and that this is becoming the new norm, thankfully. This has come as we as a society have ensured better chances for women in all fields and can also be attributed to the likes of Young Warriors, Jazz re:freshed and more recently Women in Jazz providing avenues for young, talented female artists".

Many institutions offering higher education are, as discussed earlier, re-evaluating their teaching of jazz and including the importance of women in the development of the art form. Nick Reynolds, Head of Jazz at of Chichester Conservatoire, says, "The jazz history modules at level five focus on how jazz created a platform for inclusivity and intercultural dialogue. At level six we look at jazz from a postmodern standpoint, which includes gender studies and women's history in jazz and how jazz, as a progressive and global art form, continues to engage with the socio-political sphere particularly with regard to inclusivity".

Nick Smart is Head of Jazz Programmes at the Royal Academy of Music and he comments, "One important thing to say is that we really do want the gender balance to improve and as far as I can see from our auditions and the Junior Jazz intake, it definitely IS improving. Not as fast as we'd like perhaps, but it does seem to be going in the right direction".

Kim Cypher believes that "it's exciting times for female performers. I would say things appear to be moving forward very positively in this respect. I am certainly more aware of growing numbers of incredible female jazz performers on the scene right now who are gaining huge respect for their music and who are very much part of the scene. This may not have been the case several years ago as I remember playing gigs/festivals where there were clearly more male performers than female. Right now, though, I think there's huge solidarity among female performers, supporting each other and moving forward with confidence".

For years, gender equality in UK jazz has been an issue and a continuing discussion in the background. Now, this subject has come to the forefront and is acknowledged as an ugly part of the art. Change is happening. It is simply a question of how to get on board, how fast that change needs to happen and how to make it stick. For society as a whole, balance is a good thing and something we aspire to. Better still, there should be an equal pool of people suitably talented and qualified so that by the simple law of averages, essentially equal numbers of men and women get selected. Gender should not be an issue – the music must remain centre stage.

What needs to happen

The research and discussions that went into this book have shown that there is an awareness that change needs to happen and there are many willing to help. Many of the answers can be found by talking to those in UK jazz and listening to their experiences and ideas. Undoubtedly change is happening, although there is also caution, but there is an awareness and enthusiasm for the jazz scene in the UK to grow and diversify. Following are some areas which need to be looked at further:

- Increasing the pool of female musicians by offering sponsored studio time and recording sessions to female-led groups and increasing their visibility by promotion. A model for this is found in Leeds where music management and promotion firm Festival Republic has launched a three-year project which provides a step up for female-led bands and solo artists as well as those wanting to work in sound production and engineering. With accommodations and travel paid for by their Rebalance programme, the selected artists will have one week's studio recording time and a slot at a Festival Republic or Live Nation festival event. The Live Nation events include jazz.

- More funding for projects in UK jazz similar to Rebalance, PRS, Arts Councils and local grants. Whilst disparity exists, these need to be targeted at female jazz players and geared towards increasing the pool and tackling gender disparity. Once this is

achieved the grants can be directed elsewhere. If the
initiatives work they should not be needed for long.

- Mentoring schemes where female (or male) jazz
  musicians take on the nurturing, advice and
  encouragement of female musicians in a
  professional setting.

- Set up more supportive networks and legislation
  including improving pay gap reporting.

- Support paternity cover and enable shared parental
  leave for those who are self-employed. Extend
  maternity protections amongst self-employed and
  freelance musicians.

- Provide greater protection against sexual
  harassment and victimisation with increased access
  to legal advice.

- Pledges by venues and record companies to support
  initiatives (like Women in Jazz and Keychange),
  and conducting audits of staff and rosters in order to
  set their own diversity targets to improve female
  recruitment, especially in leadership roles.

- Encouraging female students to play traditionally
  "masculine" instruments and join jazz ensembles.

- Encouraging women to have high quality
  photographs and text, and to insist this is used in

publicity. Providing more workshops on how to present oneself professionally, to disallow stereotypical representation in the media.

- Encouraging more women to write about jazz.

- Funding more studies of the gender disparity and reasons why it exists.

Should these items be achieved even partially, the resulting discourse should lead to further discussions and action.

Jazz has, as part of its music, a heap of traditions, practices and behaviours, many of which perpetuate the lesser importance of women. Historical elements will get lost but maybe they need to go.

There is no magic way to have 50:50 parity in UK jazz overnight. Even with blind auditions, the number of men auditioning would far outweigh that of women, making it much more likely more men would get selected. It's not there are too many men either, just not enough women.

UK jazz has to embrace change and take opportunities for positive forward-thinking. There is, in UK jazz, the opportunity to lead by example. Women want it, men want it, the youth want it, so it will happen.

David Jones of Serious (who curates the London Jazz Festival) once explained that female jazz players have it tough because at college, they are constantly in a place where they are a minority, they can be shut out and socially there are limited opportunities for networking because nearly everyone else is male. This is changing slowly and hopefully more females will be able to study jazz as part of their degree or as their major subject.

Male musicians have greater opportunities to network because there are simply more of them. If they connect with someone and do not get on or it does not work out, they can move on. For a woman, this is more difficult because if she works with another female musician and it does not work out, who is she going to move on to? It will more than likely be a man.

As I brought the information together in preparation for this book, I was aware of a paradox. On the one hand, it is easy to find musicians who feel there is gender disparity in UK jazz on a large scale and action is needed before the scene becomes too distanced from its audiences. On the other hand, there are also musicians, male and female, who feel progress is being made. There are academics who believe huge advances have been made both in education, performance and the media's representation of women in UK jazz.

Those positive aspirations are commendable but a look at festival line-up figures, observations from venue managers and educators and the experiences of many musicians, which will tell you that the reality for many is very different from theoretical resolutions.

There is undoubtedly a general desire for lasting change on all sides. The issues are being tackled piecemeal and each part is important, but until the pieces come together to provide a holistic and encompassing equality, and gender disparity becomes a rare topic in conversation, there is work still to be done.

Increased awareness of disparity where it exists and the desire to address it is a good thing. It creates a positive and harmonious atmosphere where no one feels belittled, sidelined or dismissed, everyone has a voice and the music is the centre of attention.

Once there is parity and equality of opportunity, we can play, consume and enjoy the music regardless of societal labels and allow jazz to speak for itself.

Further reading

Books

Alkyer, Frank and Enright Ed. "DownBeat: The Great Jazz Interviews". Publisher: Hal Leonard ISBN 978-1-4234-6384-9 (2009).

Campbell, James. "The Picador Book of Blues and Jazz". Publisher: Picador, ISBN 978-0-330-32755-8 (1995).

Cooke, Mervyn. "Jazz (World of Art)". Publisher: Thames and Hudson, ISBN 978-0-5002-0318-7 (1999).

McKay, George. "Circular Breathing: The Cultural Politics of Jazz in Britain". Publisher: Duke University Press, ISBN 978-0-8223-3573-3 (2005).

Stein, Sammy. "All That's Jazz". Publisher: Tomahawk Press, ISBN 978-0-9557670-9-8 (2017).

Stein Sammy. "Women in Jazz". Publisher: 8th House, ISBN 978-1-926716-55-8 (2019).

Articles, Blogs, Papers

Bain, Vick. "It's the Brits! Awards & Festival Line-Ups: The Pipeline Problem", Music Ally Ltd. (2020). https://musically.com/2020/02/19/music-gender-representation-and-the-pipeline-problem/

Björck, Cecilia and Bergman, Åsa. "Making Women in Jazz Visible: Negotiating Discourses of Unity and Diversity in Sweden and the US", IASPM Journal (International Association for the Study of Popular Music), Vol. 8, No. 1 (2018). https://iaspmjournal.net/index.php/IASPM_Journal/articl e/view/878

Caudwell, Jayne. "Jazzwomen: Music, Sound, Gender, and Sexuality", The Annals of Leisure Research, Vol. 15 (2012). https://www.tandfonline.com/doi/full/10.1080/11745398.20 12.744275?src=recsys

Conway, Colleen. "Gender and Musical Instrument Choice: A Phenomenological Investigation", Bulletin of the Council for Research in Music Education No. 146 (2000). https://www.researchgate.net/publication/298596122_Gend er_and_musical_instrument_choice_A_phenomenological_ investigation

Creech, Andrea. "Perceptions of Leadership Progression Pathways & Nurturing Aspiring Female Jazz Leaders" (pdf), The Institute of Education, University of London (2014). https://nationalyouthjazz.co.uk/gender-research/report/

Johnson, Christopher M. and Stewart, Erin E. "Effect of Sex Identification on Instrument Assignment by Band Directors", Journal of Research in Music Education, Vol. 52 (2004). https://www.jstor.org/stable/3345435?seq=1

Koenig, Anne. "Comparing Prescriptive and Descriptive Gender Stereotypes About Children, Adults, and the Elderly", Frontiers in Psychology (2018). https://www.frontiersin.org/articles/10.3389/fpsyg.2018.01086/full

McKeage, Kathleen M. "Where are All the Girls? Women in Collegiate Instrumental Jazz", GEMS: Gender Education, Music and Society Journal, Vol. 7 (2014). https://ojs.library.queensu.ca/index.php/gems/article/view/5207

Millard, Marie. "Five Things to Teach Your Female Students About Jazz", Brass Chicks (2018). https://www.brasschicks.com/2018/10/06/five-things-to-teach-your-female-students-about-jazz/

Parsonage, Catherine and Dyson, Kathy. "The History of Women in Jazz in Britain"; Chiti, Patricia Adkins, ed. ("Women in Jazz/Donne in Jazz"), Rome: Editore Columbo, pp. 129-140 (2007). http://oro.open.ac.uk/19391/

Provost, Sarah C. "Bringing Something New: Female Jazz Instrumentalists' Use of Imitation and Masculinity", Jazz Perspectives, Vol. 10 (2018). https://www.tandfonline.com/doi/abs/10.1080/17494060.2018.1443966

Valenti, Talya. "A Study to Investigate the Participation of Female Jazz-Trained Instrumentalists at WAAPA and in Perth's Professional Music Scene" (pdf), Thesis, Edith Cowan University (2018).

https://ro.ecu.edu.au/cgi/viewcontent.cgi?article=2522&context=theses_hons

Wehr-Flower, Erin. "Differences Between Male and Females' Confidence Anxiety and Attitude Towards Learning Jazz Improvisation", Journal of Music Education, Vol 54. (Winter 2006).
https://www.researchgate.net/publication/240725657_Differences_Between_Male_and_Female_Students'_Confidence_Anxiety_and_Attitude_Toward_Learning_Jazz_Improvisation

Wehr-Flowers, Erin. "Understanding the Experiences of Women in Jazz: a Suggested Model", International Journal of Music Education (2015).
https://journals.sagepub.com/doi/10.1177/0255761415619392

Useful Contacts and Links

Arts Council
https://www.artscouncil.org.uk/funding/project–grants–supporting–grassroots–live–music#section–1

The Equality Act
https://www.legislation.gov.uk/ukpga/2010/15/part/2/chapter/1

The F-List
https://vbain.co.uk/the–f–list

Girl Plays Jazz
https://girlplaysjazz.org.uk/about/

Help Musicians
https://www.europejazz.net

Higher Education Statistics Authority
https://www.hesa.ac.uk/

International Women in Jazz
http://www.internationalwomeninjazz.org/

Jazz North
https://www.jazznorth.org/jazz–camp–for–girls

Jazz South
https://jazzsouth.org.uk

Jerwood
https://jerwood.org/about

Keychange
https://keychange.eu/

New Youth Music
https://new.youthmusic.org.uk

Sandy Brown list
https://www.sandybrownjazz.co.uk/Features/UKJazzFestiv
als2019.html

She Is the Music
https://sheisthemusic.org/

SHE SAID SO
https://www.shesaid.so/

Sisters in Jazz
http://jazzednet.org/sisters-in-jazz/

Trinity Laban
https://www.trinitylaban.ac.uk/

Tomorrow's Warriors Female Frontline
https://tomorrowswarriors.org/tw–female–frontline/

Universal Production Music
https://www.universalproductionmusic.com/en-gb/campaigns/100her-she-said-so

We Have Voice
http://www.wehavevoice.org/

Other Resources

33Jazz RPM www.33jazz.com/catalog

Debbie Burke's jazz blog www.debbieburkeauthor.com

The Conversation – "Why is There So Little Space for Women in Jazz Music?" https://theconversation.com/why–is–there–so–little–space– for–women–in–jazz–music–79181

The Guardian – "Blind Auditions in Orchestras and Gender Bias" https://www.theguardian.com/women–in–leadership/2013/oct/14/blind–auditions–orchestras–gender–bias

Lionel Shriver piece in The Spectator – "Jazz is Dominated by Men: So What?"
https://www.spectator.co.uk/article/jazz-is-dominated-by-men-so-what-

List of organisations that advocate for diversity in music
https://www.composerdiversity.com/advocates

The National Jazz Preservation, Education, and Promulgation Act of 2017
https://www.congress.gov/bill/115th–congress/house–bill/4626?s=1&r=6

Time and Leisure – "Where are the Women in Music?"
https://www.timeandleisure.co.uk/where–are–the–women–in–music

Value in Live Music – The UK Live Music Census 2017 report by Emma Webster, Matt Brennan, Adam Behr, Martin Cloonan and Jake Ansell
https://livemusicexchange.org/resources/valuing-live-music-uk-live-music-census-report-2017-emma-webster-matt-brennan-adam-behr-and-martin-cloonan-with-jake-ansell-2018/

Vick Bain – "The Gender Pay-Gap in Music"
https://vbain.co.uk/blog/f/the–gender–pay–gap–in–music

Photographers

Several photographers were generous enough to provide photos of musician and events:

Phil Barnes https://blueblueneonglow.wordpress.com/

Colin Black https://colinblackphotography.com/

Ron Milsom https://www.ronmilsomphotography.com/

Jacques Redmond ("Gender Disparity in UK Jazz" cover design)

Malcolm Sinclair https://www.pbase.com/malco/root

Acknowledgements

I wish to thank the individual photographers who gave permission for the use of their work in this book.

Without the help of many people who have researched, worked in and played jazz music in the UK over many years, I would not have been able to write this book. The information on UK jazz and women in UK jazz in particular is scant and not holistic so having their cooperation has been invaluable. In no particular order, I'd like to acknowledge the following:

Catherine Tackley who allowed me to use her research work for the *Women in UK Jazz* historical section.

Vick Bain, researcher, industry consultant and campaigner, who allowed me extensive use of her research and thoughts.

Andrea Vicari, professorial staff at Trinity Laban, researcher and composer, who gave me access and allowed me to use her research.

To the men and women of the UK jazz scene, the writers, performers, educators, record labels and researchers not included in this list who gave their time, thought, suggestions and support I give huge thanks. This book has brought together information from a variety of sources and the cooperation and support from everyone has been immense. Thank you.

INDEX

ABOUT THE COVER

Top row, from left to right:
Alison Affleck by Colin Black, Charlotte Keeffe by Robert
Crowley, Kat Lee Ryan by John Sutton

Second row:
Yazz Ahmed by Seb JJ Peters, Helen Papaioannou by Phil
Barnes, Joy Ellis by Adam Osmianski

Third row:
Jo Harrop by Malcolm Sinclair

Fourth row:
Millicent Stephenson by Keri Hunt

Fifth row:
Debbie Burke by Donna Lynn Photography, Juliet Kelly by
Malcolm Sinclair, Kim Cypher by Ron Milsom

Sixth row:
Trish Clowes by John Cronin, Tamar Osborn by Steve
Thompson, Emma Fisk by Malcolm Sinclair

BIOS

Sammy Stein is a popular reviewer, author and columnist, writing for three columns where she brings her keen analysis and eye for detail. She has reviewed music by Sting, Bowie, Monk, Coltrane, Binker & Moses, Mats Gustafsson, Claire Cope, Tina May and many jazz musicians. Her book "All That's Jazz" (Tomahawk Press) received critical acclaim and her "Women in Jazz" (8th House) gained the Jazz Times Distaff Award, made the Gearbox list and was nominated by the Jazz Journalists Association for best jazz book. Comments included "What an incredible book" (*Phace Magazine*); "It really is an intelligent, insightful and consistently entertaining read" (*Ian Mann, Jazzmann Reviews)* and "It's all here, beautifully written, eloquently argued, clear-eyed in its intentions and open in its invitation" (*Jane Cornwell, Jazzwise*). She has curated several radio series, been on Jazz FM, BBC, Jazz Bites Radio and more. Sammy organised the London Jazz Platform mini-festival event. She was named the Jazz Journalists Association International Editor by the Jazz Journalists Association. For more information visit www.sammystein.org.

Debbie Burke (editor) is an award-winning editor and author whose jazz blog has earned international praise. Her other books include "Icarus Flies Home", "Tasty Jazz Jams for Our Times", "Glissando: A Story of Love, Lust and Jazz", "The Poconos in B Flat" and "Music in the Scriptures". She is also the owner of Queen Esther Publishing LLC. For more information visit

www.debbieburkeauthor.com and
www.queenestherpublishing.com.

Printed in Poland
by Amazon Fulfillment
Poland Sp. z o.o., Wrocław

63564500R00121